I0234406

REVERSE THE ARROWS

SENDING THE CHURCH BACK TO THE NEW TESTAMENT

Wyatt House books may be ordered through booksellers or by contacting:

WYATT HOUSE PUBLISHING
399 Lakeview Dr. W.
Mobile, Alabama 36695
www.wyattpublishing.com
editor@wyattpublishing.com

Because of the dynamic nature of the Internet, any web address or links contained in this book may have changed since publication and may no longer be valid.

Cover design by: Nick Trentham

Interior design by: Mark Wyatt

ISBN 13:978-1-954798-13-7

Printed in the United States of America

REVERSE THE ARROWS

SENDING THE CHURCH BACK TO THE NEW TESTAMENT

MATT DAY

WHP

Wyatt House Publishing
Mobile, Alabama

DEDICATION

To every Pastor...

CONTENTS

Chapter 1

SOUND THE ALARM

Do you know what is happening right now with the traditional Church in the Western world? It's shrinking at an alarming rate. The statistics are in about the current state of the Church and its people, and they are not good. For instance:

What percentage of the U.S. population attended an evangelical, orthodox church in 1990? 20.4%. What percentage of the U.S. population attends an evangelical, orthodox church today? 14-15%.

In that same time frame, the general population of the U.S. went from 250 million to 330 million, an increase of 24% or 80 million people. The population has rapidly increased by 24% while the churched population has decreased by 6% in that same time frame.

This information has sent church researchers into a frenzy, waving giant red flags as if to say that if nothing is done, evangelical church attendance will be in the single digit percentage in the United States by 2050. We can't keep doing what we've been doing!

Ed Stetzer, president of the SBC research arm says, "This is not a blip. This is a trend, and the trend is one of decline." [1]

What's so alarming about all of this is that these are all pre-Covid statistics! What has become apparent with the effects of Covid-19 on the Church is that these statistics are already out of date. Not only does this gap exist, it has been drastically widened beyond anyone's imagination.

What Covid-19 has done to the Church is to show us what the gap was going to look like in 30 to 50 years. However, instead of taking it decades of time, slowly inching toward these numbers, Covid accelerated these numbers, and it only took one year to do it! Church strategists are now telling Pastors that 30-36% of people who once attended a church building on a regular basis will never come back. [2]

Some church analysts are going so far to say that they firmly believe that 1 in 5 churches are facing permanent closure within 18 months because of the pandemic. [3]

According to a recent Gallup poll, for the first time in recent American history, church attendance has fallen below 50%. [4]

Barna Research for April and May 2020, showed that *"among practicing Christians—those who identify as Christian, agree strongly that faith is very important in their lives and attend church at least monthly (prior to COVID-19)—over half (53%) say they have streamed their regular church online within the past four weeks. Another 34 percent admits to streaming a different church service online other than their own, essentially 'church hopping' digitally. Finally, about one-third of practicing Christians (32%) say they have done neither of these things."* [5]

I've met with Pastors who have said,

"Our numbers are down from 3,000 to 1,700. Everything is being re-evaluated. We are basically starting over."

"We are starting over and only keeping what is necessary."

"I know of congregations that have lost 10,000 people and they are scrambling about what to do."

"I've discovered many of the people in my church are unconverted. They are cultural Christians."

Maybe you are a Pastor reading this, and you are thinking similar things, or maybe for the first time, you are looking around and feeling frustrated and overwhelmed as you look at the current model.

Let me tell you, it's not a bad thing to begin thinking differently. As a matter of fact, I believe this is exactly what the Lord wants us to do.

Not including COVID-19, why do you think the percentage of church attendance before COVID was rapidly declining? Let me give you an illustration. Picture the faces of people who look totally uninterested in being a part of a local church. They don't think about attending. They are happy to sleep in on the weekends, happy to keep their hard-earned money in their pockets and spend their time filling it up with whatever they want to do. The local church to them is irrelevant. What percentage of the population have I just described?

Think about a second face. It's the faces of people who are angry. They are angry at the Church for hurting them or abusing them. Maybe they felt forced to go as a child and no longer want to subject themselves or their children to that. Maybe from the outside looking in they see scandals. They see *"brainwashed"* people, or they see the Church as nothing but a scheme to take people's money, and because of that, they are angry at the Church. What percentage of the population have I described?

Let me give you a third face. It's the faces of people who have tears streaming down their face. They love Jesus, they just don't love His Church. Maybe they've been a part of a church body in which there was a lot of conflict. Maybe they saw an abuse of power. Maybe they saw their local church becoming political or more of a business. Maybe they felt unappreciated or unnoticed. For whatever reason, they still love Jesus, but they are not in love with the Church and are scared to jump back into another one. What percentage of the population have I described?

An *"I don't care about the Church"* face, an *"I'm angry at the Church"* face, and an *"I'm sad about the Church"* face. These faces are real, and a lot of people have these faces, more than we realize.

Joshua Packard, author of the book *Church Refugees*, coined the term *"Dones"* to describe those who were burned out on ministry and fed up with organized religion. The people in his study were not people who had walked away from one bad church experience. Many in the study had tried out at least four churches over a tenure of many years and many did not want to leave. Why did they leave the traditional church? I can come up with some reasons as to why they did:

Their church had become too political or powerful.

Their church had become more of a business rather than a body, or a corporation rather than a community.

Their church had become more about entertainment rather than evangelism.

They got hurt or wounded and treated badly.

Maybe there was a scandal in their church that left them disillusioned.

Maybe they just wanted something more out of their church, like something was missing.

One person interviewed in the article put it like this, *"I guess the church just sort of churched the church out of me."* [6]

Because of Covid, now more people than ever are starting to think like this. They may not be able to articulate it, but they know that something's not right with the current model of Church, and there are definitely things that are not right.

According to Carey Nieuwhof, (pre-Covid statistics) 94% of churches aren't growing or aren't growing as fast as their communities, and barely 1 out of 20 churches are effectively reaching their neighbors for Jesus. [7]

9% of those who claim to be born again, tithe. [8]

In my Friday morning Bible study, someone in our group threw this out, *"Billy Graham believed that 80-85% of those who attend church are lost. They have never been saved."* When that was presented to our Bible study group, the rest of the group nodded their heads in agreement, believing that statement to be totally true.

I sat there shocked, and I said so. I wanted to make sure that every person in the group understood to what they were agreeing. I wanted them to understand that if Billy Graham's statistic is true, then our current model of Church has failed us.

Think about a business that manufactures goods, and 85% of what came out of their factory was wrong, tainted, or printed incorrectly. That business would not remain open for very long, and I believe we are headed down this path as the Church in the United States.

Recently I asked a group of Christians who had been walking with the Lord for 30 or 40+ years this question: *"Have you reached maturity?"* Everyone in that room shook his or her head *"No"* emphatically. They were nowhere near maturity in their estimation. I was a bit shocked and I'm sure the expression on my face said so.

According to the most recent study, 6% of the U.S. population possesses a Biblical worldview.

A Biblical worldview is described by George Barna as:

"Believing that absolute moral truth exists; that such truth is defined by the Bible, and firm belief in the six specific religious views. Those views are that Jesus Christ lived a sinless life; God is the all-powerful and all-knowing Creator of the universe and He still rules it today; salvation is a gift from God and cannot be earned; Satan is real; a Christian has a responsibility to share their faith in Christ with other people; and the Bible is accurate in all of its teachings." [9]

6% of Americans today believe this. *"Born again Christians"* were three times more likely than average to have a Biblical worldview at 18%.[10] But listen, that still means that 82% of professing *"born again believers"* don't have a Biblical worldview!

What's even more startling, according to this recent study on Biblical worldviews by the Arizona Christian University Cultural Research Center, is that their research has shown that only 37% of Pastors have a Biblical worldview! [11]

There's something radically wrong with what was just stated. This is the real pandemic that we are facing! No wonder one of the Pastors that I talked with during the pandemic stated that he believed many of the people attending his church are actually lost. Many are just *"cultural Christians,"* with no sense of the indwelling Holy Spirit invading and wrecking their lives.

This is why we can't continue to do what we've always done. Covid-19 has taught us to think differently, and it's time that we started doing so.

When I was writing this during the Covid-19 pandemic, church buildings were shut down, people were quarantined in their homes and businesses were closed. It was a very strange time in which to live. Someone posted on social media during that time a picture of an empty church auditorium with the caption, *"The Church has left the building."* I thought, *"Shouldn't this have always been the case?"* Maybe this is God's sovereign way of doing just that. I firmly believe that it is.

[1] John S. Dickerson, *The Great Evangelical Recession*, (Baker Books; Illustrated edition, 2013), 32.

[2] Tony Morgan, *Q3 2020 Unstuck Church Report*, www.unstuckgroup.com.

[3] Michael Gryboski, *1 in 5 Churches Facing Permanent Closure Withing 18 Months Due to Covid-19 Shutdowns*, (The Christian Post, August 26, 2020). www.christian-post.com.

[4] Jeffrey M. Jones, *U.S. Church Membership Falls Below Majority for First Time*, (Gallup News, March 29, 2021). www.news.gallup.com.

[5] George Barna, *State of the Church*, (July 8, 2020). www.barna.com.

[6] Joshua Packard, *Meet The 'Dones,'* (Christianity Today, 2015). www.christianityto-day.com.

[7] Outreach Magazine, *7 Startling Facts: An Up Close Look at Church Attendance in America*, (Outreach Magazine, April 10, 2018). www.churchleaders.com.

[8] George Barna, *New Study Shows Trends in Tithing and Donating*, (April 14, 2008). www.barna.com.

[9] George Barna, *A Biblical Worldview Has a Radical Effect on a Person's Life*, (December 3, 2005). www.barna.com.

[10] George Barna, Arizona Christian University Cultural Research Center, *American Worldview Inventory*, (October 6, 2020). www.arizonachristian.edu.

[11] Ibid.

Chapter 2

THE MARCHING ORDERS OF THE CHURCH

Does anyone see a huge problem with everything that I've just shared with you? The Church in the U.S. in rapid decline? Believers not maturing? Some Pastors believing that *"cultural Christians"* are filling up their churches?

"Okay, Pastor Matt. I receive what you are saying, but what can be done about this? What should the Church and its people be doing?" I'm so glad you asked that question!

The mission of the Church has never changed. Every church body that names the name of Christ has the same mission. That mission may be expressed in unique ways or specific ways, but it is the same mission none the less. *"Pastor Matt, what is the mission of the Church?"*

Is it FELLOWSHIP: The gathering of the saints of God together to enjoy the company of the Lord and of one another? It's important, but that's not the mission.

Is it TEACHING: Teaching correct doctrine, expounding on the Truth found in the Word of God? Again, important, but that's not the mission.

Is it SINGING: The Church body gathered together, raising voices collectively in a chorus of praise to our matchless Savior? Important, yes, but not the mission.

The mission, the marching orders for every church body and every person in every Bible believing church body is found in Matthew 28.

Then Jesus came to them and said, "All authority in heaven and on earth has been given to me. [19] *Therefore go and make disciples of all nations, baptizing them in the name of the Father and of the Son and of the Holy Spirit,* [20] *and teaching them to obey everything I have commanded you. And surely I am with you always, to the very end of the age"* (Matthew 28:18-20, NIV).

At this point in the story of Matthew's Gospel account, Jesus has just been raised from the dead. He has appeared to the women attending His tomb, and He tells these women to tell His disciples to meet Him in Galilee.

Here they are at this meeting. The Resurrected Christ has requested the presence of His disciples and has appeared to them to meet with them. What is He going to tell them? What's the mountaintop thing that He's about to say to them?

Is He going to tell them that He is about restore Israel politically?

Is He about to tell them His plan for sweeping the totality of evil off the planet?

Is He going to tell them that He is about to start a holy war on this earth?

In this mountaintop moment with His followers, He gives them one command:

Make Disciples

This is the singular mission that Jesus gave to His followers then and now. That's it. This is the mission that Jesus left for us to do. Make disciples.

I was recently talking with an associate Pastor of a church body in my area and explaining to him the vision of my church which is all about reversing the arrows, which I will explain a little later in the book. He was fascinated as I shared this Biblical understanding of Church with him.

When he got back to his office, he snapped a picture of his bulletin board and texted it to me. Then we talked. He said, *"What's on that bulletin board is on my heart. It's a strategy for making disciples in our area. But, do you know the one thing that my job won't allow me to do? Make disciples."*

I said, *"Why?"*

Do you know what he said to me? *"What would I do for a living? How would I provide for my family? Besides, I have to prepare the hospitality station and get things ready for the people walking through the doors of our church building who are already saved."* As he shared his heart with me, he did so with tears rolling down his face. Sadly, I'm afraid he's not alone in his tears when it comes to the Lord's bride.

Let me give you some general observations about this passage that we call *"The Great Commission."* The passage is set off by the word *"ALL."* Jesus says that **all** authority has been given to Him. We are to go into **all** nations, teaching them to obey **all** things. As we go, Jesus promises to be with us **always**.

ALL authority,

ALL nations,

ALL commands,

ALWAYS,

ALL believers,

ALL places.

Understand that if you claim to be a follower of Christ, this mission applies to you. It applies to ALL who name the name of Jesus, but as we've seen in the previous chapter, the Church in the United States is shrinking. The obvious conclusion to that glaring problem is that the command to *"make disciples"* is not being carried out by every person.

Let me ask you, what is the reason behind the call to go and make disciples? What is at stake if we disobey this command of Jesus? Look at Matthew 28:18 again.

Then Jesus came to them and said, "All authority in heaven and on earth has been given to me. Therefore go and make disciples..." (Matthew 28:18-19a, NIV).

The Authority of Jesus

Jesus says that all authority in heaven and on earth has been given to Him. It is the authority of Jesus that is the compelling reason to make disciples. The reason we go and make disciples is because the authority of Jesus is at stake.

Let's understand what this statement really is. It is a declaration of kingship. It describes a totality of rule. It speaks of a universal kingdom and a universal rule. *"All authority in heaven and on earth has been given to Me."*

There is no power above the Lord Jesus Christ, and there is nothing too far reaching from His authority. He is the reigning, conquering, King. It is not a reign as an earthly political king but a reign that is spiritual, able to conquer evil and subdue and rule in the wayward heart of man.

His declaration of authority is actually the fulfillment and realization of Daniel 7.

"As my vision continued that night, I saw someone like a son of man coming with the clouds of heaven. He approached the Ancient One and was led into his presence. [14] He was given authority, honor, and sovereignty over all the nations of the world, so that people of every race and nation and language would obey him. His rule is eternal—it will never end. His kingdom will never be destroyed" (Daniel 7:13-14, NLT).

This is what Jesus has in mind, and this is what Jesus is alluding to when He makes this declaration of authority. It is so that every race, nation and language would fall under His realm of obedience.

What then does He do with this authority? He gives that authority to us! Let's understand this in two ways:

1. *He Directs His Children*

"Go and make disciples. Expand the Kingdom so that My house will be full."

2. *He Declares His Heart*

By saying, *"Go and make disciples,"* He is essentially declaring that He wants every person to be a part of His Kingdom. The Lord of the Nations longs for every people of every nation to come under the authority of His good reign, AND He orders every Christ-follower to engage in that endeavor.

Why? Why does He want every person to be a part of His Kingdom? Is it because He loves people? Yes. John 3:16 tells us that.

Is it because He doesn't want anyone to go to Hell? Yes. But there is a specific, highly motivating reason behind the call to make disciples, and it is found in 2 Corinthians 4.

"We know that God, who raised the Lord Jesus, will also raise us with Jesus and present us to himself together with you. [15] *All of this is for your benefit. And as God's grace reaches more and more people, there will be great thanksgiving, and God will receive more and more glory.* [16] *That is why we never give up..."* (2 Corinthians 4:14-16a, NLT).

The ultimate reason to never give up is so that people from every tribe, language, and nation can come under the authoritative rule and reign of Christ and His kingdom and give Him THANKS so that He can receive more and more GLORY!

Do you know about the 10/40 window (10 degrees north and 40 degrees north latitude)? The 10/40 Window is the rectangular area on the globe that stretches from North Africa through the Middle East to Asia. Why is this area important?

This is where majority of unreached people groups live—meaning they have never even heard the name of Jesus. It's a massive group of people consisting of approximately 5 billion individuals in 68 countries. Do you know what percentage of missionary funding goes to reaching these unreached people? 1%. [2]

Most of our mission funding and missionary endeavors goes towards working among the already reached people groups! This doesn't seem right, does it? All nations means all nations, and Jesus expects us to go.

I praise God for Phil and Elin Henderson. Phil and Elin answered the call to go to the unreached nations, and they went. They partnered with *Ethnos 360* and went to an unreached people group in Mozambique, a group of 200,000 who are predominately Muslim.

Phil and Elin learned Portuguese, the official language of Mozambique, but quickly realized that the people they went to reach not only did not speak Portuguese but also did not have their native language in written form! Having no house, no land, no understanding of the language, and knowing not a soul on that part of planet earth, they went.

They learned the native language, captured the language on paper by creating an alphabet, and taught the people how to read their own language using the only thing that was in print—the translated portion of the New Testament done by Phil.

When my wife and I went to visit them, we sat down under a shade tree with these new believers. They were reading the book of 1 Corinthians for the very first time in the history of their civilization!

Not long after we left, forty of these believers followed the Lord in believer's baptism. Again, this is a Muslim country we are talking about. Others, from two hours away, are begging people from this tribe to come and teach their tribe the Word of God. Phil and Elin heard the call, and this group of people is now giving thanks and praise to Jesus because of it!

I love the quote by John Piper which says, *"Missions exists because worship does not."*[2] This is the primary motivation behind making disciples. It is so that more and more people can join with the chorus of Heaven, giving thanks and praise to God as they come under the perfect and gracious rule and reign of Christ and enter His Kingdom of Light.

Imagine Jesus making a secret appearance on this earth. It's in a 100,000 seat stadium, and you find out about it. You are so excited, yet when you get there, you notice that only 1,500 people have come to see Jesus. Angrily you say to yourself, *"This is not right! He deserves the worship of the entire world!* (AND HE DOES). *Why aren't more people here?"*

The reason why we tell people the Good News about Christ is so that we can gather an army of people to stop worshipping themselves and the things of this world so that they can erupt in a magnanimous chorus of praise and thanksgiving to God for all eternity who is worthy!

When the people of this earth don't do that, we rob God of receiving glory and praise. Do you understand that? This is why the Apostle Paul says, "THIS IS WHY WE NEVER GIVE UP."

When you think about your salvation story and how you were rescued by God, do you not say, *"Thank you?"* Do you not stand and applaud and say, *"Thank you, God, for saving ME?"*

God wants the Kingdom of His Dear Son to be ever expanding and ever reaching, and He says to us, *"MAKE DISCIPLES AS YOU GO TO THE ENDS OF THE EARTH."*

As you go to the coffee shop,

As you go to your children,

As you go to your neighbor across the street,

As you go to your mother or father,

As you go to your classmates,

As you go to the farthest unreached people group on the planet.

As you go, make disciples so that more and more people can give worship and thanksgiving to the glorious Lamb who was slain and to the One who sits on the throne!

God does not waste opportunities, nor does He do things randomly. He has purpose in everything He does, including Covid-19. Could it be that God is desperately trying to get the attention of the Church in America? Could it be that He is not wanting the Church to go back to *"normal?"* Could it be that He is trying desperately to get His bride to mature and to send her out?

This is exactly what He did to the believers in the New Testament. God sovereignly caused the Church of the New Testament to scatter. You find that in Acts chapter 8. They wanted to stay in Jerusalem, worship Him at the Temple and enjoy the fellowship and goodwill of the people. They wanted *"Heaven on earth,"* but God had different plans.

How did He cause the early Church to scatter? Through persecution, terror, hardship and trial, all accomplished by the hand of the Apostle Paul.

What was involved in the scattering? Loss of homes? Loss of jobs? Loss of family? Loss of belongings? When it hit, they had no time to pack or make arrangements. This was difficult, and this was inconvenient. Unlike us living in the West, they had no rights. They couldn't demand a hearing in a court of law. It was either flee, or be dragged to jail or die.

What did that scattering do? It spread the Church out and placed the believers all over the Mediterranean. Look at Acts 8:4. Don't miss this.

"But the believers who were scattered preached the Good News about Jesus wherever they went" (Acts 8:4, NLT).

And from Acts chapter 8 on, you see the Church spreading out. What is interesting is that the disciples, before the Holy Spirit was given to them, go from primarily being called *"disciples"* or *"learners"* to *"Apostles"* which means *"one who is sent."*

Let me ask you: Was the scattering of the Church in Acts chapter 8 the devil's doing or God's sovereign hand? Did the devil send persecution or did the Lord? God sovereignly did this to the early Church, and I believe He wants to do it again.

We are not to stay cloistered in the safety of our church buildings and experience *"Heaven on earth."* We are to make disciples and work and toil until all people know and come under the gracious rule of Christ so that He can receive the most praise and receive the most glory!

[1] Radical Staff, *The Unreached Should Receive More Than One Percent*, (July 6, 2021). www.radical.net.

[2] John Piper, *Let The Nations Be Glad*, (Baker Academic, 2010), 1

Chapter 3

SEEING THE CHURCH WITH FRESH EYES

What if it's our system of Church that is the problem? *"What do you mean?"*

In 2015, I started feeling restless in my first and only pastorate. I had been there for 10 years, and it had been the only church I had ever pastored.

There were several emotions stirring within me at this point in my life. I had an intense longing to be closer to family. We were living in South Florida, in a beautiful place, right along the Gulf of Mexico. Sounds like paradise, but my immediate family was ten hours away and my wife's family was fifteen hours away which included grandparents, brothers and sisters, nieces and nephews, and aunts and uncles. Being away from family with four small kids was weighing on me. My kids were growing up without their immediate family to watch them do so.

I was confused. Do I stay at my current position and continue pastoring this growing church or do I put my resume' out and see what else is out there closer to home? When I contacted churches, there seemed to be little to no interest on their behalf. Also, no churches were contacting me. None.

I also was a frustrated visionary. I had been wearily pastoring a church that had moved locations over fifteen times around the city and never had a permanent facility. We looked at several properties and buildings but those doors were closed every single time. So, we met on Sunday mornings or Sunday nights or Saturday nights. We met outside, in schools, in shopping plazas, in performing arts centers, and in city venues. Our slogan quickly became, *"If you can find us, you can worship with us."*

During this time of wandering, I began to wonder about my leadership. *"Lord, is it me? Am I missing something? Why can't we find a permanent place to meet? Lord, we want to experience Your glory. Why can't we have a building?"*

To me, not having a permanent place was the one roadblock in my mind that was keeping us from exploding in growth. People were already driving long distances to come to our services. We had people in attendance from an hour away, an hour and a half away, and two hours away, coming from many different directions in Florida. A permanent location would give us stability and allow us to launch out into other areas. So I thought.

One morning in November of 2017, I had a candid conversation with God. I walked around the office park where the office space that we rented was located. In my prayer that morning, I pleaded with God, *"Lord, for two years I've been restless. Either fulfill this desire to be closer to family or take it away."* It was as if a lightning bolt had hit me. He answered my prayer by immediately taking away my desire to be closer to family.

I had become rejuvenated to keep on serving in my current position. I no longer had an overwhelming desire to be near family. I actually used to dread set up and tear down as a mobile church. Right then, I looked forward to it. I couldn't wait for Sunday to come. I committed myself to the Lord at that moment and said that if He wanted to keep me here, pastoring this one and only church for the rest of my life, I would gladly do it!

This mind mountain of having to have a building in order to move on to the next step was also removed by God. He made it very clear to me that we didn't need a building in order to move forward. *"Don't wait for a building. Move forward with what I've called you to do."* But how? I needed clearer direction.

Not long after that I had a conversation with a woman in our church. *"Have you heard of this Church in Austin, Texas?"* (she named the church). *"They are a mobile church that looks a lot like our church, that has planted several campuses throughout the city."* It was a short conversation but one that startled me. How did she know what was going on in my heart? I had never heard of an intentionally mobile church that went ahead and planted other campus locations. I felt compelled to go to that church in Austin and check it out for myself.

That next Sunday, I jotted down this new vision on a piece of paper, right before I was about to go on the platform to preach. *"We will plant campuses throughout Southwest, Florida even as a mobile church."* I wrote down names of people who could lead worship at these campuses, people who could preach at these campuses and people who could lead at these campuses. I didn't know how any of this could be accomplished, but I knew that I had direction from the Lord.

At this point, I told the elders of the church everything: my restlessness over the years to be closer to family, my frustration as a visionary, how the Lord had changed my heart, about the church in Austin. They were surprised at my wanting to leave but relieved at my determination to stay.

Several of us decided to make the trip to Austin, Texas to see this church. We went to the *"live"* venue first, then we made the trip across town to one of the *"video"* venues to experience what that was like. It was new to us, but we walked away excited.

We all agreed that this would be the direction of our church, and we made steps to send it in that direction. At this point, I had put a building out of my mind. We didn't need it any more in order to move forward. We had our heading. If the Lord wanted to bless us with a building, then that was His business, but we were not going to wait for a building to get started.

In my personal time with the Lord during that period, God had shown me this passage in Joshua: *"Reap what you did not plant. Occupy what you did not build."* What did that mean? I was sure that a building for our church was up to God, and we were to let God take care of that. If He wanted it, He would provide it for us. If not, we were to move ahead with what He called us to do.

In 2018, I began to sense a restlessness among the elders. They wanted this vision but they also wanted a building. Within months, the vision had clearly shifted: building first, planting a campus second, and by the end of that year right before Christmas, I was fired from my first and only pastorate. I had served there for almost 14 years.

My wife wondered at the time if a Pastor can be fired from a pastorate for anything other than being *"unpastoral."* I also wondered the same thing, however, I submitted to their decision. If they did not want me there, I did not want to be there.

Even though it was a hurtful and crushing experience for us to walk through, and even though there was much confusion around that ordeal because we didn't know what the Lord was up to, we soon came to realize that I was fired, not for anything I had done, but fired by the sovereign hand of God. Some have called it *"promotion by firing."* Promotion from God rarely looks anything like we think it should. This was definitely one of those moments.

Here I was, finally thinking that I had a clear direction from the Lord, only to find out that I'm terminated. I thought the desire to be nearer to family was taken away, and yet now I'm out of a job? When it happened, I was so confused. I couldn't sleep, and I couldn't eat, and I had nowhere else to go but to crawl into the lap of Jesus and seek comfort from Him.

"Lord, where are You in this? I have four kids. What am I going to do? How am I going to provide for my family? Is this Your way of getting me close to my family? I thought You had taken that desire away from me. What about the vision You gave me? What am I supposed to do

about that now?" I had so many questions and no real answers. I desperately needed the Lord to speak.

Do you know that when you are desperate for the Lord, that's who you get? Many of us really don't reach that level of desperation. We usually don't need the Lord for the "*trivial"* things of this life, but when you are desperate for the Lord to speak, wanting nothing else, He answers.

He conveyed to my wife and I early on in this ordeal to *"Be still and wait patiently for Me to act."* At every turn we faced, we kept seeing and hearing this phrase: in the Bible, on a coffee cup, listening to the radio and many other ways. However, what the Lord said to me when I was curled up in His lap as I lay face down on my bed was different.

I distinctly remember Him saying to my heart when I came to Him with all these questions,

"I called you to preach."

I countered. *"Yes, Lord, but you have to be invited to preach at places. You can't just show up and preach."*

"I called you to preach."

"Lord, like into a video camera?"

"I called you to preach."

Then I thought, *"If I preached into a video camera, I could preach five times a day! I wouldn't have to wait on an invitation!"*

It was at that point that I took out a legal pad and began to write out this clear vision for Church that I am going to share with you, which is the basis for reversing the arrows. I wrote down page after page of what I believed the Lord was downloading to me, helping me to see the Church with new eyes as if a blindfold had been ripped off of me.

It wasn't until God opened my eyes to the pattern of Scripture through this ordeal, that I began seeing things in a different light. It was pain in my life that brought me to Him. It was Him that brought me to this, and when I received it, it was like I was literally born again.

In the presence of God, I opened my Bible and read the New Testament with fresh eyes. I saw the system of how the early Church was done. I saw the pattern that was used in building the Church, and the characteristics that had marked the Church. I had not seen this before. I had only seen what I already knew about Church, but this was different. This was new. This was real. What exactly did I see?

I kept asking myself this question. *"Does the Church today look like the New Testament Church?"* When I would ask this question to Pastors and mature believers, many would start shaking their head *"No"* before I even finished the question. My next question was always the same. *"Then why do we continue to do it this way?"* They look at me as if to say, *"We don't know any other way, or we are scared to do anything differently."*

What if we began thinking differently? What if COVID-19 is God's way of forcing us to think differently?

As God began opening the New Testament to me in a way that I had never experienced before, I began seeing a reversal of the arrows from how we typically do church. Let me explain what I mean.

Instead of people leaving their neighborhood on Sunday mornings and driving to different churches around the city, what if we reversed the arrows and sent everything that is experienced in a typical church service (worship, preaching) to those people right where they are in order to set up their house, apartment, office, etc. as a local church in the center of all of the lost and hurting people living right around them?

We could turn houses, coffee shops, schools, offices, huts into churches and resource them to be the local church right where they are! Not an inflow into a building but an outflow from the church building into where we live and work and where the people who need it most are. This is what was meant by the passage in Joshua: *"Reap what you did not plant. Occupy what you did not build."* We could use all the things that are already built!

When I explained this concept to the Pastor that I grew up under for the first 21 years of my life, his eyes grew big. I said, *"Brother Fred. We had about ten thousand people in our church growing up and a four thousand seat auditorium. What if one Sunday you stood on the platform and said these words:"*

'Don't come back to this building next week. Instead, pick up a sign on your way out that says, "Cottage Hill Baptist Church Meets Right Here" and plant it in your front yard. Get to know, minister to, pray with, help, serve, love on, and invite over to your dining room table all the people who live around you. Mow their grass, bake them cookies, serve them and love them in Jesus Name'."

I then said, *"What if you gathered them all back in one month and told them to bring with them all the people that they ministered to? How big of a building would you need?"*

He said, *"Matt, we couldn't build a big enough building."*

I then said, *"Brother Fred. That's only after one month! Imagine doing that month after month!"*

Do you know what he told me? He said, *"Matt, this is the future of Church. I wish I was forty years old again. I would do church exactly as you have described it."*

Brother Fred Wolfe at that time was 82 years old and has sense gone to be with the Lord, but he caught the vision of what it could look like for the Church to reverse the arrows.

When I told another Pastor my vision for church, he got more and more excited to the point of yelling at me. *"Pastor, Matt. You have to write this down! You have to let Pastors know all about this! Where did you get this? How did you come to this information? Promise me you will write this down!"*

What you hold in your hand, is the answer to that plea.

During this time of restlessness of wanting to be closer to family, I was also having a difficult time with my elder board. Elder boards can be tricky. You can start to see *"godly"* men turn into *"business"* men really fast. At one point during this frustrating time with the elders, I drove to a parking lot and told the Lord that I had made up my mind to stand before the congregation the following Sunday and announce my resignation. I was done. Do you know what the Lord told me in that moment? *"You can do that, but the devil will receive the victory."* I was stunned. I quickly changed my mind and told the Lord that I didn't want the devil to receive any victory from my life. Not long after that, I was fired.

For a long time after my firing, I struggled with this conversation. If the devil was not to receive any victory, how was I now out of the pulpit? Didn't he get what he wanted? Didn't he indeed receive the victory by my firing? I had one Pastor reach out to me and tell me that I was such a target of spiritual warfare that the devil had to take me out. Is this what happened?

I didn't receive clarity about this until years later. Here's what I realized. The victory was not in me staying in my role as Senior Pastor. That was not the victory at all. The victory was in showing me, what I'm now giving you in this book. This was the victory, and here is the reality of that situation. I had to walk though that painful time of being treated like a criminal in my firing with lies being spoken about me and *"friends"* walking away from me in order for God to reveal this concept of reversing the arrows.

I went to lunch with a friend after I was fired, and I told him about what God had revealed to me in the New Testament, which is the basis for this book. He said to me during this lunch, *"Pastor Matt, do you think you would have received anything from the Lord like you did had you not gone through that trying time exactly as you did?"* I told him, *"No."* Had I never walked through that painful experience, I would have never known about reversing the arrows. This is the true victory that the Lord wanted to show me.

Chapter 4

WHAT IF THERE IS SOMETHING DIFFERENT?

Let me tell you first what was made keenly aware to me as I looked freshly into the New Testament. The term *"Church"* in the New Testament never refers to a building or a place but rather to a BODY. The BODY of believers.

The Definition of Church

Church actually means, *"The called out ones unto the Lord."* It speaks of the people of God, not a place. Do you know where the Church primarily and solely met for the first three hundred years of its existence? In homes.

"And Apphia our sister and Archippus our fellow soldier, and the church in your ***house****"* (Philemon 1:2, ESV, emphasis mine).

"And day by day, attending the temple together and breaking bread in their ***homes****, they received their food with glad and generous hearts,"* (Acts 2:46, ESV, emphasis mine).

"The churches of Asia send you greetings. Aquila and Prisca, together with the church in their ***house****, send you hearty greetings in the Lord"* (1 Corinthians 16:19, ESV, emphasis mine).

"And every day, in the temple and from ***house to house****, they did not cease teaching and preaching Jesus as the Christ"* (Acts 5:42, ESV, emphasis mine).

"Greet also the church in their ***house****. Greet my beloved Epaenetus, who was the first convert to Christ in Asia"* (Romans 16:5, ESV, emphasis mine).

"I commend to you our sister Phoebe, a servant of the church at Cenchreae, [2] that you may welcome her in the Lord in a way worthy of the saints, and help her in whatever she may need from you, for she has been a patron of many and of myself as well. [3] Greet Prisca and Aquila, my fellow workers in Christ Jesus, [4] who risked their necks for my life, to whom not only I give thanks but all the churches of the Gentiles give thanks as well. [5] Greet also the church in their ***house****"* (Romans 16:1-5, ESV, emphasis mine).

"Give my greetings to the brothers at Laodicea, and to Nympha and the church in her ***house"*** (Colossians 4:15, ESV, emphasis mine).

Whether it was because of persecution throughout the Roman Empire or because of Jewish persecution that forced them into homes, the fact remains that homes were the predominate places of worship throughout the New Testament. Why?

Christianity in the Roman Empire was illegal. It was treason to worship another deity other than the Emperor, and if you were a Jew, you were enraged for worship to be given to anyone but the One True God, Yahweh.

If followers of the Way were found out, they were persecuted, dragged off to prison and killed. The Apostle Paul tells us this in many places in Scripture, but especially as he stands before King Agrippa.

"I used to believe that I ought to do everything I could to oppose the very name of Jesus the Nazarene. [10] Indeed, I did just that in Jerusalem. Authorized by the leading priests, I caused many believers there to be sent to prison. And I cast my vote against them when they were condemned to death. [11] Many times I had them punished in the synagogues to get them to curse Jesus. I was so violently opposed to them that I even chased them down in foreign cities" (Acts 26:9-11, NLT).

I think it is fascinating that the one who caused the Church to scatter through persecution was also the one who caused the Church to spread through preaching! Even though this was an intense time of persecution, the Church spread throughout the Roman Empire.

Why is this important? Why is important to understand that the Church solely met in homes, in small groups?

With the only place of gathering in the New Testament being in homes, this means that every one of the commands in the New Testament, every one of the ordinances in the New Testament and every one of the interactions in the New Testament has to be seen through the lens of a small group of people gathered. That is all they had available as an option for the first 300 years of its existence.

Let me go over that again very carefully.

Every one of the commands in the letters of the Apostle Paul dealing with accountability, discipleship, discipline, worship, gathering, spiritual gifts, giving, etc. and every one of the interactions the Apostle Paul had, must be seen through the lens of a small group of people gathered.

It is only when you see it through this lens that the New Testament makes sense in terms of maturity and discipleship. It is no wonder God was already working on my heart while I was still pastoring my church. *"You don't need a building. Move forward with what I've called you to do."* This vision was not given to the church I pastored. I now know that. It was given to me to give it to the whole body of Christ.

Today's Definition of Church

When we say the word *"Church,"* what do we mean? For many people, that means *"go to church"* or *"go to a church building."* When you ask someone about a church, what's usually your first question? *"Where do you go to church?"*

But let me ask you, when does the New Testament use the language, *"go to church?"* For a culture that uses that expression very often, the New Testament does not. Remember, there were no buildings when the New Testament was written. There were no churches called *"First Baptist Ephesus"* or *"First Methodist Philippi"* or *"First Pentecostal Thessalon-iki."* Anything that existed, existed underground away from the watching eyes of the Roman Empire.

When the New Testament talks about a church, it always refers to a people—*"the called out ones unto the Lord."* Therefore, according to the Scriptures, we don't *"go to church"* but rather we ARE the Church. We are the people of God.

The best way to understand the word *"church"* in a Biblical sense is to substitute the word *"church"* for *"body."* You would never say *"I go to body."* Nor would you say, pointing to a church building, *"That's my body."* You would say, *"I gather WITH the body"* or *"That is WHERE my body meets."* The early church hearing us speak today would ask us, *"How can you go to something that you are?"*

The closet concept to understanding how the New Testament Church functioned is found in the context of a small group of believers sharing life and doing life together in community. This is something that I never saw before reading Scripture.

Micro vs Macro

In 2019, I talked with a church staff in Texas that was willing to listen to my vision for church and help me refine it. When I was with them, I asked them these questions:

"In your city, if everyone came under the conviction of the Holy Spirit and decided to attend a church building in your city on the same Sunday, would there be enough seats in all the churches to hold all the people in your city?"

They emphatically told me, *"No."*

I asked a follow up question. *"What percentage of the city could fit in all the seats of all the churches at the same time?"*

It was something they had never thought of before. *"Fifteen to twenty percent."*

I asked them another question. *"How many people in this city have a place to lay their head tonight that they either rent or own?"*

"Ninety-five to ninety-nine percent."

This is when their eyes got really wide, and you could visibly hear them catch the vision.

If every residence, every restaurant, every building became a gathering place for believers, the options would be unlimited. We wouldn't have to build anything, but simply use everything that is already built.

The point of what God gave me through the reading of the New Testament and through the understanding of reversing the arrows is that what we have to know going forward is that the future of the Church as we know it will not be in temples that we *"go to"* but rather around the tables that we transform into church gatherings.

Table Not Temple

As I read through the New Testament, I also saw the model of the Church. What do I mean? Let me ask you this, *"When you think about 'Church' today, what do you primarily think of?"* Sunday morning? Church building? Seated in rows listening to someone on a platform?

If you were to ask the New Testament believers that same question, what would they say? The dining room table. The primary discipleship method in the early Church was around a dining room table, and there are examples of this all over the New Testament.

Paul talks about a meal in 1 Corinthians 11 and calls it *"The Lord's Supper."* (We are going to look at this in more detail in a later chapter.) When you look at church discipline, what does the New Testament often say? *"Don't eat with him." "Don't fellowship with him."*

The dining room table was the centerpiece for discipleship, accountability and fellowship, just like it should be in every family home today. How did I miss this? In this environment, people can't hide.

Think about twenty people in a small group versus two thousand people in a traditional church. In which model is accountability more functional? In a traditional model, it's easy to blend in, arrive late, leave early and never really be known or seen. It can often be a great place to hide. But, think about accountability in the context of a dining room table. You can't hide.

If you don't show up, everyone will know it. If you are having marital problems, everyone will know about it. Don't, however, let this thought intimidate you! It's exactly what the New Testament has in mind when it comes to church! The understanding of the dining room table also works for spiritual gifts, spiritual disciplines, helping people become more like Jesus, and taking care of the needs of others. The New Testament Church functions in community, and community is best understood in the context of a dining room table. We will look at this in more detail in a few chapters later.

The Priesthood of Believers

Something else that I failed to see clearly was the priesthood of the believer. I knew it existed but I didn't know how to fully grasp it.

Let's start with the Apostle Paul. What was his system of church planting in the New Testament? He traveled from place to place preaching about the Resurrection of Jesus. When he arrived at a place, he would reason in the synagogue with the Jews first. When they no longer wanted to hear what he had to say, he would then turn to the Gentiles and reason with them. It never failed that some always responded to the Gospel. It was with these people that a church body was formed. Paul would stay there and help them, sometimes for years as in Ephesus and Corinth. Other times he was run out of town that very night by angry Jews. This was his similar pattern.

Leaders were soon raised up from these believer groups that helped Paul spread the Gospel. They were not seminary trained Pastors. They didn't have seminaries back then. They didn't even have a copy of the New Testament like we do today, and they did not have children's Pastors or student Pastors to help them. They were ordinary people who relied on the Holy Spirit to govern their every move.

Heavenly Minded

Lastly, what I saw with the understanding of reversing the arrows is the mindset of the early believers. They did not live for the pleasures of this earthly life but for the life to come. They saw their houses and property and even their own lives as not their own.

They moved with a heavenly mindset. People traveled all over the Aegean Sea. Timothy traveled extensively with Paul. Titus was sent to Crete. Apollos was in Ephesus and then in Corinth. Aquilla and Pricilla were in Corinth and then in Ephesus. Luke traveled with Paul and documented his journey. There were people with Paul in Rome while he was in prison, as well as many other examples.

They were focused on going more than anything else. Is this what you find in our churches today? I'm going to expound on this later in the book, but I believe this is what God wants the Church to get back to, reversing the arrows back to the original design of the early Church.

When I was released from my former church, a dear lady gave me a verse. She did not know that I was starting this movement in 2020, but she gave me ACTS 20:20 which is where the Apostle Paul is speaking to the Ephesian elders.

"I never shrank back from telling you what you needed to hear, either publicly or in your homes" (Act 20:20, NLT).

Publicly and in our homes. This is what the New Testament had in mind from the very beginning! Why did God call me to start this movement back towards the New Testament in 2020? I thought, initially, it was to bring the Church back to 20/20 vision regarding the New Testament. Little did I know that the year 2020 would be a marked point in human history, with people quarantined in their homes and church buildings sitting empty. During this time, people from all over began texting me when they heard about my church planting movement. *"How did you know about Covid-19? How did you know to start churches in homes?"* I told them that I didn't know, but that I was just obeying what God had told me to do.

God wants His Church to be released. May *"publicly or in your homes"* be the anthem of the Church moving forward, and may this verse be brought to full expression as we reverse the arrows.

Chapter 5

A GIANT SHIFT

The church that I grew up in was wonderful. I was shaped and molded in that church. God's presence seemed to hover over that place. This was my understanding of church. In my mind, this is how church was to be done, and that's how I tried to pattern the church that I pastored. We had a building in the church that I grew up in, therefore my church needed a building. Preaching was central, therefore preaching needed to be central in my church. People came, sat in rows and listened to the Pastor powerfully speak. That's what I thought church was supposed to be.

If you think about churches today, many of them are patterned after what we experienced growing up. They may look a little different or have a different style of music but the general pattern is the same: Sunday morning, seated in rows, listening to a person speak.

How did we get our current pattern of church? If the early Church didn't look this and couldn't look like what we have today, from where did it come?

Constantine

I've often thought about early Christian life in the Roman Empire. What real rights did Christians have? When Nero burned down most of Rome, on whom did he place the blame? Christians. Think about what's happening in Communist China right now. Pastors have no real rights. Every day they face the possibility of imprisonment or abduction because of false charges leveled against them.

In 2017, a prominent Chinese lawyer named Gao Zhisheng, who advocated for imprisoned and persecuted Pastors, was abducted by the Communist Chinese government and has never been found.

I met one Chinese Pastor who told me that he had been imprisoned twenty-five times. His wife had been tortured for *"withholding information"* about their church while being chained to a chair. He told me that when he returns back to his church in China, the authorities have already requested to meet with him for another interrogation.

The fastest growing church right now (2023) is said to be in Islamic Iran. Do you think Christians there are treated with favor and have rights? No, the people there are afraid, every day, and fearful that someone will turn them in. If that happens, they will face torture, imprisonment, banishment from family, or death, yet they don't care! For them, telling others the wonderful news that Jesus saves is all that matters, and thousands and thousands of Muslims are turning to Jesus for salvation.

This is the backdrop of the early Church. Now, let's think about this for one second. If you were living in that time, having no real rights, living on the bottom rung of society in people's minds, and a *"Christian"* Emperor ascended the throne, what would you be thinking? Yes! Finally!

Enter Constantine. In 324, Constantine became emperor of the entire Roman Empire. What did *"Christian"* Constantine do for Christians living at that time? He gave them lots of privileges including the right to assemble without fear. He even built church buildings all over the Roman Empire: Jerusalem, Bethlehem, Laodicea, Constantinople, and Rome to name a few. This is the first introduction of church buildings into the Christian scene. The fourth century.

What did these buildings look like? They were buildings worthy of a Roman Emperor. Think about it. Constantine was steeped in Roman culture. He patterned the churches that he built after what he saw in Roman architecture and after what he experienced in Roman life. He had the authority to build whatever structure he wanted. He was the Roman Emperor after all!

Structures during that time brought *"legitimacy"* to the movement. Pagans have sacred Temples, Jews have sacred Temples, therefore, Christians needed sacred Temples.

When I first traveled to Ephesus, I saw Greek gods everywhere. I mean, everywhere. The goddess of victory (Nike) stood over you as you entered the city. The Starbucks logo is chiseled into one of the monuments. There were memorials to all kinds of gods and emperors all along the main road leading to the Celsus Library. Paul's description in Acts 17 of what he saw in Athens, *"To an unknown god,"* really hit me as I walked down that road. There were gods everywhere in Ephesus.

There were so many sacred shrines dedicated to the worship pagan gods that I literally became sick to my stomach as I saw the totality of them. This was the world of the early Church and this was the world of Constantine, entrenched with pagan and Roman influence.

His churches were built in the same way as the Roman basilica. The basilica was the main gathering place for watching performances. They were built for the masses as well as government officials and magistrates, and those two groups of people did not mingle.

In Constantine's Christian basilicas, there were elevated steps and platforms where the clergy ministered, away from the people. There was also a rail or a screen that separated the clergy from the *"laity,"* an idea that is never found in Scripture. Remember? Priesthood of ALL believers!

There was also an altar, placed in the middle of the basilica. The altar was considered the most holy place in the building because it usually held the relics of some saint. By the fifth century, a church was considered legitimate only if it had a relic.

When I went into several of the monasteries and church buildings in Greece, what did I notice? A shrine in a prominent place in the building, housing the encased skull or some other body part of a deceased saint. As we were observing these *"holy places,"* worshippers would come in, bow and kiss the glass of the container that held the relics.

What else was placed on the altar in Constantine's basilica model? The holy eucharist or communion. Only the holy men were allowed to handle the holy eucharist, but where is this found in the letters of the Apostle Paul?

In front of the altar was the Bishop's Chair, *ex cathedra.* Ex cathedra means *"from the throne."* It was modeled after the seat of the judge in the Roman basilica. From that seat, a message was given along with the authority of the Church declared. Around the chair sat the elders and deacons in a semi-circle.

In Ephesus, we visited the Basilica of Saint John, built by Emperor Justinian in the 6th century. Hardly any of the structure still stands, but the Apostle John is believed to be buried there. I don't know for sure, even though presumably I stood over his tomb. What I did notice was the remaining structure of the basilica that surrounded the tomb. It still had a raised platform where the clergy was supposed to sit during the service, elevated and away from the people. Every Pastor in our group was asked to sit there for a picture.

The Basilica of Saint John was designed and patterned after the Church of the Holy Apostles in Constantinople, one of the earliest Christian basilicas built by Constantine. What's interesting about The Church of the Holy Apostles building, even though it no longer exists, is that it appears to have been built as a shrine to Constantine! When he built it, he placed shrines to the twelve apostles, surrounding a single tomb, which lay at the center. That tomb was reserved for Constantine himself, as some have said, making him the 13th and chief apostle! [1]

Because the Emperor was the most significant person in the Church, he had to have special privileges like his own entrance.

When I walked into the Hagia Sofia church building in Istanbul (Constantinople), I encountered something interesting. I noticed a giant door that served as the main entrance into interior of the church building. Our guide told us, *"That's the Emperor's entrance. Only the Emperor could enter through that door."* That's when it dawned on me. The Roman Emperor was not only a member of the church but was also the Roman Emperor while he was a member of the church! Think about his membership. Are you really going to tell the Roman Emperor you can't do this or that? He's the Emperor who built you a building!

I also learned that Emperors customarily had lights carried before them whenever they appeared in public. Constantine brought this custom into the Church. He also brought in the practice of having the clergy dress in special garments, just like the Roman officials.

The Christian basilica, which was built to house the Emperor, was also seen, in itself, as a holy and pure sight. When we walked through Laodicea, I was asked a question by our guide that I couldn't answer. As a matter of fact, no one in our group could answer the question rightly. She told us that we were standing outside of the basilica that Constantine built in Laodicea.

You could see the mosaic floor that was still somewhat intact even though multiple earthquakes had ravaged the area. Then she asked, *"What is this?"* pointing to a trough of some sort that was sitting outside of the entrance into the basilica.

"Baptismal?"

"No."

That was all we could come up with. Then she told us.

"It was used for ceremonial washing before you enter inside."

None of us as evangelical Christians, literally from all over the world, made that connection. But, for our Muslim guide (the only guides in Turkey are all Muslim) this made perfect sense. Let me explain.

When I was in Mozambique, I had the chance to go to one of the African mosques in one of the villages. The local Imam, Edrisa, was a friend of Phil Henderson and was part of his Bible translation team, helping to translate the New Testament into the language of the people! Explain that one!

When Edrisa took us to the mosque, he demonstrated the ceremonial washing that had to take place before you could enter in. Right ear, left ear, right hand, left hand, and on and on he went. *"When you walk into the mosque, you have to step in with your right foot and exit the mosque with your left foot."*

My wife asked him when we were done, *"Do you still believe what's taught in this mosque?"* He replied, *"Some things I do, some things I don't."* The Gospel was clearly taking root in his heart. He died a few years later. There is no doubt in my mind that I will see him in heaven.

What did our Muslim guide in Laodicea think about the ceremonial washing station outside of the *"Christian"* church? *"Ah, Christianity is just like Islam. We follow the traditions of Mohammed, you follow the traditions of Jesus."*

During our trip, I pulled her aside and told her how ceremonial washing was not found in the New Testament. I'm not sure she understood.

It was Constantine who also began making the clergy a paid position. He paid the clergy nice salaries, in addition to being exempt from serving in the military and from paying taxes. How many people do you think wanted that job? Sign me up!

One other thing about Constantine that you need to know is that he never gave up worshipping the sun-god. He wrote into law in 321 that every Sunday (Sun-day) was to be a dedicated day of rest. *"On the ven-*

erable day of the Sun let the magistrates and people residing in cities rest, and let all workshops be closed." [2]

This was not a dedication to the Son, as in the Son of God, but the Sun as the Roman god. This Sunday law, no doubt, was an obvious introduction of pagan sun worship into Christianity.

Do you see the huge predicament the early Church faced? *"The Emperor is on our side! This is an act of God!"* Yet everything in Scripture opposes the world's systems and any contact with paganism. It appears that we are still today facing that same predicament today.

Constantine introduced into the Christian culture in the 4th century, a lot of paganism and a lot of power. There was now a clear confusion regarding that which is holy and that which is not and that which is clergy and that which is laity, again, an idea that is never found in the New Testament.

Our guide in Greece was amazing. He was a true believer in Christ and probably one of the smartest people I have ever met. Because he speaks Greek, he reads his Bible in the original Greek language! I asked him about Constantine and what he thought about the impact of Constantine upon Christianity. His reply is one that I will never forget.

"The devil tried to destroy the Church through persecution. Instead, he married the Church through Constantine."

Let that sink in. The devil married the Church through Emperor Constantine! When I first went to Turkey and Greece, I saw lots of things. I went to many Biblical places mentioned in the book of Revelation and in Paul's letters. Guess what I didn't see in all the places that I visited? The early Church. There was no physical trace of the early Church anywhere. The only evidence of the early Church that you see today is the evidence of its lasting impact as it turned the world upside down.

Can it be that way again? Could it be that God is forcing us to walk this path of maturity and discipleship? It will take the body of Christ, specifically Pastors, divorcing what they currently know of church, reversing the arrows, and going back to the system of church found in the New Testament, free from the rule of Emperor Constantine.

[1] Frank Viola and George Barna, *Pagan Christianity? Exploring The Roots of Our Church Practices, Revised and Updated.* (Tyndale House Publishers, 2008), 19.

[2] *Codex Justinianus* lib. 3, tit. 12, 3; trans. in Philip Schaff, *History of the Christian Church, Vol. 3,* (Sagwan Press, 2015) 380, note 1.

Chapter 6

THE CHURCH HAS BEEN HIJACKED

Because Constantine had such a dramatic influence on Christendom since the 4th century, his influence is still being carried out today. Picture this: The Church was heading in an upward trajectory and Constantine sent it into a right angle. That's how dramatic the shift was from what was done in the early Church for the first three hundred years.

That is what Constantine caused it to do, and it's been traveling in that direction ever since. Many of us, without even knowing it, are still bowing to Emperor Constantine to this very day. Let me give you some examples.

Sacred Spaces

As we read earlier, Constantine gave the understanding that the Christian basilica was *"sacred"* or *"holy."* The space housed the Holy Roman Emperor, and it housed the holy communion, the *"presence of the Lord."* You see the hand washing purification process still being observed in many traditional churches today. There are bowls of water in the back of the building for you to wash your hands in. It shouts very loudly to all that enter, *"This place is holy. You must purify yourselves before you come in."*

"Well, we don't see our building that way. It is just a place where we meet." Let me push back on that a bit.

How many times have you or someone else thought or said, *"We are going to 'God's House'"* or *"We are going to meet God?"* If you were taken to a church building as a little kid, how many times did your mother tell you to act right because you were in *"God's house?"* How many times did you hear, *"There is no running in the house of God"* or *"There is no gum chewing in the house of God?" "There must be complete reverence."*

When the Pastor or worship leader gets up to speak to the audience, what did you often hear often coming from his mouth? *"Isn't it so good to be in the house of God this morning, amen?"* or *"Don't you love seeing God's house full?"* We still treat the building as sacred.

What is sacred according to the New Testament understanding?

No More Sacred Spaces; Every Person Is a Sacred Temple

"Don't you realize that your body is the temple of the Holy Spirit, who lives in you and was given to you by God? You do not belong to yourself, for God bought you with a high price. So you must honor God with your body" (1 Corinthians 6:19-20, NLT).

The Holy Spirit who is God, dwells IN US. He has not promised to dwell in a building. That's an Old Testament understanding. He's promised to dwell in every person who names the name of Christ. According to the New Testament, we are His Temple!

Sacred Dress

When I was little, I asked my mom why we dress up for Sunday morning church. Her reply is probably what a lot of moms have said over the years. *"We dress up because we want to give the Lord our best."* But, as I grew up, I never really understood that idea in regards to Monday. *"What about Monday? Is Monday not also a day to give God our best?"* This kind of thinking carries the idea, whether we intend it or not, that one day is special above all others and that God really cares about that one day.

Let's talk about the priest or the minister. Does your minister wear special clothing when he stands before the congregation? Why does he wear these special garments? It's rooted in two areas. The priesthood garments found in the Old Testament and the garments of the Greco-Roman world. [1]

During the reign of Constantine, the Bishop's dress was in the same fashion as the ancient robe of a Roman magistrate. Throughout the years, the dress became more and more elaborate for a priest: from white in the 4th century to purple in the 5th century, to more costly garments in the 6th. In the Middle Ages, the clothing had taken on a new level of elaborate decoration full of mystical and symbolic meanings.

This is why, during the Protestant Reformation, the Reformers preferred the long, black scholar's gown. Before long, this became the garment of the protestant Pastor, and many protestant Pastors still wear that gown.

Let's think about this critically. Just off the top of your head, what does the wearing of *"best"* clothes do in the minds of people? It creates distinctions, the haves and the have nots. *"Wow, look at what she's wearing. They must be rich. Sit here in this special spot"* or, *"I can't believe they would let their kids walk in here looking like that."*

It becomes more of a fashion show or who's who in the *"house of God."* Have you ever thought, *"I'm not going to church today, I have nothing to wear?"* This is why many church bodies today are telling people to *"come as you are"* into their places of worship. They know that clothing can be a big barrier in the minds of people. James, the brother of Jesus knew this all too well.

"My dear brothers and sisters, how can you claim to have faith in our glorious Lord Jesus Christ if you favor some people over others? [2] For example, suppose someone comes into your meeting dressed in fancy clothes and expensive jewelry, and another comes in who is poor and dressed in dirty clothes. [3] If you give special attention and a good seat to the rich person, but you say to the poor one, "You can stand over there, or else sit on the floor"—well, [4] doesn't this discrimination show that your judgments are guided by evil motives?" (James 2:1-4, NLT).

Think again about the minister wearing a robe. What does that automatically do for him? It sets him apart. It conveys a message that says that he's different, distinct, and special. What does the congregation begin to think? *"He's God's man. He's the priest that stands in between God and the people. His spiritual gift is the most important."*

I don't think that any Pastor would willfully acknowledge that his gift is better or higher than anyone else's or that he is better or higher than anyone else, at least I hope not! But, I think the unintentional consequences of how we dress communicates an entirely different message than what the New Testament says.

What is the New Testament understanding?

No More Sacred Dress, We Are Dressed In The Righteousness of Jesus

A great exchange happened when you put your trust in the sacrificial work of Christ on the cross. All of your dirty sinfulness was charged to Jesus' account. Jesus was put to death and endured the wrath of God because of your sin and my sin.

But, something else happened on the cross. All of Jesus' righteousness was charged to your account when you believed. All of His perfect obedience and perfect righteousness while He lived on this earth was given to you and charged to your ledger. That's the great exchange!

This means that at this very moment, every true child of God is seen by Him as completely and fully righteous, dressed and clothed with the righteous robe of Jesus. This is what Isaiah alludes to when he writes about the future Kingdom:

"I delight greatly in the LORD; my soul rejoices in my God. For he has clothed me with garments of salvation and arrayed me in a robe of his righteousness, as a bridegroom adorns his head like a priest, and as a bride adorns herself with her jewels" (Isaiah 61:10, NIV).

No more condemnation! No more guilt! No more shame! No more sin to atone for! Forgiven! Fully and utterly forgiven!

The Apostle Paul talks about this over and over in his letter to the Romans.

"When people work, their wages are not a gift, but something they have earned. [5] But people are counted as righteous, not because of their work, but because of their faith in God who forgives sinners" (Romans 4:4-5, NLT).

"But God showed his great love for us by sending Christ to die for us while we were still sinners. [9] And since we have been made right in God's sight by the blood of Christ, he will certainly save us from God's condemnation" (Romans 5:8-9, NLT).

A fully forgiven sinner who is now counted as fully righteousness, dressed in the righteousness of Jesus. This is the New Testament's understanding of our true garments before the Lord. Spiritually covered with the righteous robe of Jesus.

Sacred Days

Have you ever heard the debate?

"Saturday is the true Sabbath. Saturday is truly the Lord's Day!"

"No. Church should be done on Sunday because Sunday is the Lord's Day. That's when the Resurrection occurred!"

Do you know what I think? I think both of these arguments are partially correct.

Let's talk about traditions for one second. What is the traditional day for Sabbath according to the Old Testament? Saturday. Jews throughout the centuries, and currently in present day, worship God on Saturday because that's the day that the Lord told them to do so.

As part of the Ten Commandments, this is what Moses told the people.

"Remember to observe the Sabbath day by keeping it holy. [9] You have six days each week for your ordinary work, [10] but the seventh day is a Sabbath day of rest dedicated to the Lord your God. On that day no one in your household may do any work. This includes you, your sons and daughters, your male and female servants, your livestock, and any foreigners living among you. [11] For in six days the Lord made the heavens, the earth, the sea, and everything in them; but on the seventh day he rested. That is why the Lord blessed the Sabbath day and set it apart as holy" (Exodus 20:8-11, NLT).

According to the Old Testament, this is still to be kept because it has no ending date. Case closed! However, when the Christian Church burst onto the scene, they began to worship on the first day of the week not on the seventh day of the week.

"On the first day of the week, we gathered with the local believers to share in the Lord's Supper" (Acts 20:7, NLT).

We know the first day to be Sunday. What changed in these Jewish men and women? The Resurrection! Jesus rose on the first day of the week.

This is why most Protestants worship on the first day of the week and call it *"the Lord's Day."*

Whether you hold fast to Saturday or hold fast to Sunday, what have we perhaps unintentionally done in the minds of the people by saying that one day is holy unto God or God receives worship on one day?

It begins to look like what I noticed on one of the music channels growing up. When I would flip past BET on the television Monday through Saturday, they put out some of the raunchiest music videos you can imagine with explicit lyrics and girls wearing barely nothing at all. Yet on Sunday, what did they play? GOSPEL music. All day! The message came across crystal clear, *"One day is for God, the rest are for me,"* and people live like this all the time.

What instead is the New Testament understanding?

No More Sacred Days; Every Day Is Sacred

Because Christ dwells within us, every day that we live is sacred unto Him, not just one day a week. Let's go back to the understanding of Sabbath. Whether you believe Saturday or Sunday is our Sabbath rest, for every Christ-follower, Jesus IS our Sabbath rest. Because Jesus rose from the dead, he conquered death and the law and fulfilled every command in the Old Testament in Himself. As believers in the Lord Jesus Christ, we no longer have to do anything to try and earn God's favor. Jesus has taken care of all of that!

"You were dead because of your sins and because your sinful nature was not yet cut away. Then God made you alive with Christ, for he forgave all our sins. [14] He canceled the record of the charges against us and took it away by nailing it to the cross. [15] In this way, he disarmed the spiritual rulers and authorities. He shamed them publicly by his victory over them on the cross.

[16] So don't let anyone condemn you for what you eat or drink, or for not celebrating ***certain holy days or new moon ceremonies***

or Sabbaths. *[17] For these rules are only shadows of the reality yet to come.* ***And Christ himself is that reality****"* (Colossians 2:13-17, NLT, emphasis mine).

We have Jesus every single day. We find our joy and our relationship IN Him. Sabbath is not just to be celebrated ONE day of the week, but in a spiritual sense it is to be celebrated EVERY day of the week because of Jesus and what He has done. This means that Jesus, who is our Sabbath Rest, can be worshiped (and should be worshipped) any and every day of the week because every day is sacred and every day is holy before Him. We must look at Sabbath with spiritual eyes and see that Jesus is the fulfillment of Sabbath.

Sacred People

Again, with the dressing up in special clothing by the minister, it conveys that only qualified people can conduct the service or handle the communion. *"Well, our minister doesn't dress up in any robe to preach to us. He just gives us the Word."* Fair enough, but does he stand in a special place in the auditorium? Yes. Where? Up front, in front of all the people on an elevated platform called a stage with the spotlight on him.

What does this do in the minds of the people? *"He's special. He's holy." "He goes up to the mountain each week to convene with God and bring down the message of God to the people, the same way that Moses brought down the Ten Commandments."* That's the expectation.

"Well, our Pastor is just a human like us, and that's how we view him." Let me push back on that just a bit. It was told to me in my firing that my position is elevated above all others and that I should be above reproach. Not the elders. Only me. Is that the expectation of Scripture? The elders who were part of my church and responsible for my firing, lied. All of them lied, repeatedly, throughout that whole situation. In the end, I was fired, but they were allowed to remain as elders, even to this day. How is this Biblical?

When my family would invite new people over to our house for dinner, they would come in nervously. They had never been in a *"Pastor's home."* One couple admitted that they were convinced that we were going to ask them to share their favorite Bible verse! Like that's all we sit around and do!

My children often felt like they were living in a glass house and were told by people, *"You shouldn't do that. You know your dad's a Pastor, right?"* Many times they resented it, and me because of it.

I worked for a Pastor when I was younger, and he told me that he could never be seen without wearing a tie. Seriously. He said that when someone knocked on the door of his home, he would jump up and race to the bedroom closet to put on a tie before answering the door!

"Are you saying that standing before the people and preaching is wrong?" Of course not! The Lord called me to preach when I was eleven years old, saying to me, *"I want you to preach."* It's five words that I will never forget. However, we have to put preaching in its proper place. It is a spiritual gift, but not the only one and not the most important one.

What instead is the New Testament understanding?

No More Sacred People; Every Believer Is Sacred

Because the Holy Spirit dwells in us, we are now sacred. I keep hearing things that I feel need to be corrected. What do we call the land where Jesus walked? *"The Holy Land."* What do we call the week commemorating the Passion of Christ? *"Holy Week."* What do many people call Sunday? *"The Lord's Day."*

I had the privilege of literally walking in numerous places where Jesus walked. I've stepped on the same stones that He stepped on. I've been inside the Church of the Holy Sepulcher where it is believed to mark the authentic places where Jesus was crucified, buried and resurrected.

How did I feel as I walked on those sites? Did I feel more holy or more connected to God? No. Did I see others in that building groveling on the floor and weeping as they touched items believed to be touched by Jesus? Yes, and it made me a little uncomfortable.

I've walked in the footsteps of the Apostle Paul. I've been in the Cave of the Apocalypse on the Island of Patmos, the place where John received his vision from Jesus that he recorded in the book of Revelation.

If you read about that place, people write that the cave is a *"holy"* place. It is known as the *"Holy Grotto."* When we walked into the cave, our first guide kept asking us, *"Can't you just feel the energy in this cave?"* I kept looking around, trying to take it all in but just found myself saying, *"I don't feel anything holy in this cave. It just feels like a cave to me."*

Let me ask you, are those stones that Jesus walked on somehow *"holy"* because Jesus walked on them? Is the Cave of the Apocalypse somehow *"holy"* because Jesus appeared to John in there? If you are inclined to say *"yes,"* read carefully the following:

There is no place on this earth more holy or sacred than that where a follower of Christ dwells at that moment.

Do you understand? The place where a follower of Jesus sits or stands is now sacred because they occupy that spot in a sacred way because the Lord is living within them! When they move, the Holy Spirit moves with them.

The Apostle Paul talks about this understanding of holiness in the context of a marriage.

"Now, I will speak to the rest of you, though I do not have a direct command from the Lord. If a fellow believer has a wife who is not a believer and she is willing to continue living with him, he must not leave her.
[13] And if a believing woman has a husband who is not a believer and he
is willing to continue living with her, she must not leave him. [14] For the
believing wife brings holiness to her marriage, and the believing husband brings holiness to his marriage. Otherwise, your children would not be holy, but now they are holy" (1 Corinthians 7:12-14, NLT).

Paul is writing to the Corinthian believers about the issue of being a believer while still being married to an unbeliever. *"What should I do? Should I now leave my spouse?"* Paul tells them that they must not leave. Why? *"For the believing wife brings holiness to her marriage, and the believing husband brings holiness to his marriage."*

Do you know what Paul is saying here? The marriage has now become holy because a person who has the Holy Spirit living on the inside of them is in that marriage. It's not the institution that is necessarily holy but the people of God who have Him living on the inside are now made holy. That's how holiness is brought into a marriage.

"You are coming to Christ, who is the living cornerstone of God's temple. He was rejected by people, but he was chosen by God for great honor. [5] And you are living stones that God is building into his spiritual temple. What's more, you are his holy priests. Through the mediation of Jesus Christ, you offer spiritual sacrifices that please God" (1 Peter 2:4-5, NLT).

"But you are not like that, for you are a chosen people. You are royal priests, a holy nation, God's very own possession. As a result, you can show others the goodness of God, for he called you out of the darkness into his wonderful light" (1 Peter 2:9, NLT).

What does Peter say about us who have trusted in Christ? He calls us *"holy priests," "royal priests"* and a *"holy nation."* We are not those things without Jesus. Far from it. But, with Jesus WE are His royal priests. Every one of us. This means that we don't have to have someone mediate for us anymore. Jesus is our Mediator, and He has cleared the way for us to have access to God, and we come to His throne as His priests, offering ourselves as sacrificial offerings to Him for His good pleasure. This is what the majority of the book of Hebrews is all about.

"So then, since we have a great High Priest who has entered heaven, Jesus the Son of God, let us hold firmly to what we believe. [15] This High Priest of ours understands our weaknesses, for he faced all of the same testings we do, yet he did not sin. [16] So let us come boldly to the throne

of our gracious God. There we will receive his mercy, and we will find grace to help us when we need it most" (Hebrews 4:14-16, NLT).

Jesus, our great High Priest has made intercession for us so that now we can come into the presence of God as holy priests, ready to offer ourselves as a living sacrifice to Him. What a picture and what a privilege! We are holy because the Holy Spirit lives in us.

Sacred Sacrifice

If you look at Communion or *"The Lord's Supper"* in the New Testament, it was done very differently than how we do it today. Very differently. In the early Church, they viewed this as a full meal. They actually called it a *"love feast,"* and Paul chastises the Corinthian church for participating in this meal with incorrect motives.

"But in the following instructions, I cannot praise you. For it sounds as if more harm than good is done when you meet together. [18] First, I hear that there are divisions among you when you meet as a church, and to some extent I believe it. [19] But, of course, there must be divisions among you so that you who have God's approval will be recognized! [20] When you meet together, you are not really interested in the Lord's Supper. [21] For some of you hurry to eat your own meal without sharing with others. As a result, some go hungry while others get drunk. [22] What? Don't you have your own homes for eating and drinking? Or do you really want to disgrace God's church and shame the poor? What am I supposed to say? Do you want me to praise you? Well, I certainly will not praise you for this!" (1 Corinthians 11:17-22, NLT).

Does this not sound like a full meal that Paul calls, *"the Lord's Supper?"* He concludes the chapter with these words:

"So, my dear brothers and sisters, when you gather for the Lord's Supper, wait for each other.

[34] If you are really hungry, eat at home so you won't bring judgment upon yourselves when you meet together. I'll give you instructions about the other matters after I arrive" (1 Corinthians 11:33-34, NLT).

If Paul describes it as a meal, when did it cease becoming a meal? The invention of the building had a lot to do with it. How do you have a community meal in a place like that?

Communion then began to take on an entirely different distinction of dread and awe. It became *"holy"* communion that only the *"holy priests"* could touch and administer. It took on a new nature so that the bread and wine actually became the body and blood of Jesus. Because of that belief, it had to be hidden away because it was too holy to look upon.

Have you ever examined the Christmas story involving Mary, Joseph and the birth of Jesus? What were you told growing up? Mary and Joseph traveled to Bethlehem for the census. There was no room for them in the Inn, so they were put out back in a stable with no one around. That's where she gave birth. In a stable with no one but the animals and Joseph to keep her company.

This, however, is the farthest thing from what really happened with the birth of Jesus according to Luke's Gospel.

"At that time the Roman emperor, Augustus, decreed that a census should be taken throughout the Roman Empire. [2] (This was the first census taken when Quirinius was governor of Syria.) [3] All returned to their own ancestral towns to register for this census. [4] And because Joseph was a descendant of King David, he had to go to Bethlehem in Judea, David's ancient home. He traveled there from the village of Nazareth in Galilee. [5] He took with him Mary, to whom he was engaged, who was now expecting a child. [6] And while they were there, the time came for her baby to be born. [7] She gave birth to her firstborn son. She wrapped him snugly in strips of cloth and laid him in a manger, because there was no lodging available for them" (Luke 2:1-7, NLT).

Later, the shepherds come to see Jesus. Much, much later, the wise men come. Okay, look at the passage. Joseph is a descendant of King David. Is that a pretty big deal? Yes. How revered was King David in the minds of the people in Israel? Hugely.

Do you think they knew who Joseph was if he was a direct descendent of King David? Do you think in a culture of honor and shame, which is still prevalent in the Middle East today, that they would have let that family be turned away at the local motel only to stay out in the cold with the smelly animals? Not on your life! They knew exactly who he was and there were probably a host of family members doting on their every request.

Further evidence is the reaction of the shepherds. They went on their way rejoicing and praising God. If there had been the injustice of a couple giving birth in an honor/shame culture with no hospitality shown to them, they would have stormed away from there mad, kicking up a fuss with every person in that village, heaping shame on them for the injustice and mistreatment of this family that has occurred.

So why has it been viewed in the traditional way of them being alone in a stable? Think about it. Mary, the *"Mother of God"* was too *"holy"* to look upon as she gave birth to the Holy One. That event, according to many, was so holy that it could not be looked upon with human eyes. Do you see how incorrect beliefs have even made their way into how we do things even today? Just look at every nativity scene.

Although most Protestants view the communion process as symbolic, they still administer it in a similar way. The bread and grape juice are on the altar. The *"holy"* ones administer it. Yet, nobody seems to be asking whether the Lord's Supper is supposed to be a real supper where real communion takes place as talked about in the Word of God or just a thimble of juice and a chicklet sized cracker. More on that later.

What then is the New Testament understanding of sacrifice?

Let me give you one verse.

"Therefore, I urge you, brothers and sisters, in view of God's mercy, to offer your bodies as a living sacrifice, holy and pleasing to God—this is your true and proper worship" (Romans 12:1, (NIV).

Our Life Is The Sacrifice That Is To Be Laid Upon The Altar

Every day and every moment of every day, we are to lay ourselves on the altar of God and say to Him, *"Burn away everything in me that doesn't look like Jesus, act like Jesus, believe like Jesus, speak like Jesus, think like Jesus and behave like Jesus, so that only Jesus can be seen in me."*

Do you understand that this is what the Christian life is all about? It is surrendering, moment by moment, to the Lordship of Jesus. Our life is the sacrifice that is to be laid upon the altar of the Lord.

Put all of this together.

We have sacred spaces, sacred dress, sacred days, sacred people, and sacred communion. Do you know what we have done without even realizing it? We have reinstituted the Old Covenant in our worship!

Sacred Space (Temple)

Sacred Dress (Priestly Garments)

Sacred Days (Sabbath)

Sacred Ministers (High Priest)

Sacred Communion (Sacrifice)

We worship God in more of an Old Testament way than a New Testament way. Think about our buildings. Think about our choirs. Think about our banners. Think about our traditions. The Holy of Holies has been ripped apart by Jesus, and we are trying desperately to sew it back up!

We are trying to encounter God in an Old Testament way by coming to the Temple and seeking His presence, but where does His promised presence now dwell? IN the lives of the very people that He has claimed for His own!

When I was in Philippi, we stood in one of the earliest church buildings that had been built shortly after Constantine came to power. You could see the transformation of the church with your own eyes. You could see that the altar first housed the Scriptures, but later became an elevated platform for the *"holy"* Eucharist, that was eventually *"hidden away"* from the congregation and put behind a divider because it was *"too holy"* to look upon.

Why It Matters

Why does all of this matter? Why is important for us to see that we are the temple of the Holy Spirit? Why is important for us to see that because the Holy Spirit dwells in us, we are sacred? Why is it important for us to see that every day is sacred before the Lord?

Because it is the people of God that make up the Church, NOT a place, NOT a building.

The sacred space is NOT the Temple we build, but rather our physical body that the Holy Spirit now lives in.

Sacred dress is NOT what we put on our physical bodies to appear righteous before God. As New Testament believers, we are perpetually clothed before God with the righteousness of Jesus.

Sacred days does NOT mean a designated day of the week set aside to worship God. Every day is sacred because Jesus is Lord of every day.

Sacred minister does NOT mean that one person is called to stand before God on behalf of the people. The New Testament clearly says that every person who has come to Christ is gifted by the Holy Spirit unto the praise and glory of God and can go right into His presence and minister unto Him.

Sacred communion is NOT a sacrifice that we put in our mouths. What God wants from everyone of His children is for us to present our bodies to Him every day as a spiritual offering of dedicated sacrifice.

I had the awesome privilege of traveling from Ephesus to Athens by boat on the Aegean Sea during the month of November. It was the last voyage of our ship for the year because of the unpredictable weather that sometimes happens on the Aegean. It was a similar route and the same time of year that Paul traveled when he was being escorted as a prisoner to stand trial before Caesar, a voyage that could have been disastrous yet for the sovereignty of God.

We must begin living out our worship with a New Testament understanding of God as priests unto Him and not an Old Testament understanding. I believe that the Lord is sovereignly orchestrating events in our present world, just like He did with Paul, to get us back to that mindset.

[1] Frank Viola and George Barna, *Pagan Christianity? Exploring The Roots of Our Church Practices, Revised and Updated.* (Tyndale House Publishers, 2008), 150-151.

Chapter 7

THE CHURCH IS NOT CHICK-FIL-A

What has the Church morphed into over the years? It has gone from a Constantinian model to a Constantinian attractional model which includes the latest sermon series, the latest lights and media creations, the latest concert feel and sound, the latest cool space, the latest kid's space, the latest sermon formats, and the latest speakers.

That was me for quite a while. I didn't know how to be anything else. Every church around me and every *"successful"* church was trying to master this attractional model. I never wavered from how I preached or the content that I preached, but I did try to be really creative and tried to create a great experience for those in attendance.

I've sense called this the *"Chick-Fil-A"* model of church: Great customer service, an inviting atmosphere, promotional giveaways and a great product—Chicken. So many churches are trying to master the attractional model with great hospitality areas, great giveaways, and a great product. They are in essence saying, *"Come try our chicken. We've got the best chicken in town,"* and what do people often do? They leave one church to try out the *"chicken"* of another.

Here's the problem. Where do you see the attractional model in the New Testament? There was nothing attractional about what the New Testament believers were offering except the Lord Jesus Christ, His forgiveness, the hope of eternal life in Him, and their lives which were built upon, influenced and radically changed by Him. Think about it.

What were they going to say to people using an attractional model? *"Come and be a part of us, the persecuted Church. Be laughed at and made fun of. Live under the constant threat of prison and death while having no rights on this earth!"*

"Yes! Sign me up for that!"

Millions of dollars are spent every year trying to make our environments more attractive. When I was still at my former church, I was invited to attend a conference on *"church growth."* I didn't really want to go, but someone paid my ticket, and I kind of felt obliged to go along. The conference was held in a huge church building in Orlando, Florida.

When I walked into the building, here's what I noticed. Thousands and thousands of theater seats. There was wood flooring on the ground, hundreds of lights in the mezzanine, and intelligent lights on the platform. I thought to myself, *"Dear, God. How much did this cost to build? 50 million? 100 million? How much does it cost to maintain the building and run the air? Is this the mission of the Church? Is this what the Church should be doing?"*

I got a pit in my stomach when I was in that building, and I believe it was put there by the Holy Spirit. This is not what He had in mind when it comes to Church. Not too long after that, I was terminated from my position as Lead Pastor.

Recently, I was talking to one of my Pastor friends. He said that he worked on staff at a church that tried desperately to add *"hype"* to their services. When God supposedly didn't move in their service like they thought He should, they went back to their staff meeting deflated trying to see what went wrong. They tried to brainstorm and add elements into their services to see if that fixed the problem. They implemented the elements into their services and wha-la, *"God"* showed up. Was it really God, or something that was manufactured by man?

Have you ever been to the wave pool at a water park? At one point the pool is calm and the next thing you know, wham! Giant waves appear. Did the waves happen because they were supernaturally moved upon? No! They were manufactured.

We've gotten so used to manufacturing *"waves"* in our churches, that it looks a lot like the real thing. Guess what happens when you begin to manufacture waves with success? You no longer need the real thing.

A.W. Tozer said this about the state of the Church in his generation. *"If the Holy Spirit was withdrawn from the Church today, 95% of what we do would go on and no one would know the difference. If the Holy Spirit was withdrawn from the New Testament Church, 95% of what they did would stop, and everybody would know the difference."* [1]

For many churches, it has become a formula. If you want to start a new campus, put in this formula and out comes four-hundred people. If you want to add more people to a service, do this. Again, it's like making and selling chicken. Season it just right, advertise it just right, pull the lever, and you get lots of customers wanting to eat your chicken. All the while, God is seemingly sitting off to the side, left out of the whole thing.

I think we need to visit Isaiah 29 once again. Look at what the Lord says to His wayward people in Jerusalem:

"For the Lord has poured out on you a spirit of deep sleep. He has closed the eyes of your prophets and visionaries" (Isaiah 29:10, NLT).

A woman from Iran had the opportunity to come to the United States with her family. By coming, she would be able to be a Christian without the fear of literal death. After a few months of being on American soil, she begged her husband to go back to Iran. *"Why? Don't you like it here? You don't have to fear death anymore."* Her reply mimicked the Lord's words in Isaiah 29.

"There is a satanic lullaby that the Church is under in the U.S., and the people in the Church are sleepy." [2]

Look at what the Lord continues to say in Isaiah 29 to the religious people of Jerusalem.

"And so the Lord says, 'These people say they are mine. They honor me with their lips, but their hearts are far from me. And their worship of me is nothing but man-made rules learned by rote'" (Isaiah 29:13, NLT).

What happens when sleepy people try to do the Lord's work? They begin worshipping Him in their own ways, using their own power.

Oh, we use His name. We say that we are His, but what would happen if He really showed up and awakened us from our spiritual stupor? What would happen to the tightly sewn up order of worship? What would happen to all the programmers wearing headsets telling everyone when to go on next? What would happen? Could it be that some churches wouldn't welcome it or would see it as an interruption to their man-made rules learned by rote?

When I was fired from my pastorate, a godly man looked at me and said, *"Ezekiel 44. That's your story."*

I thought to myself, *"Ezekiel 44? What's in Ezekiel 44? Who gives Ezekiel 44 as an encouraging passage of Scripture?"*

Let me give you some background to the book of Ezekiel. Ezekiel is a priest and prophet of God, calling out the sins of the people and the priesthood. In chapter 11, the glory and presence of God departs because of sin. In chapter 43, the glory returns.

In Ezekiel 44, God calls out the priesthood. He lays at their feet the reason why the glory, His presence, departed from the Temple.

"And the men of the tribe of Levi who abandoned me when Israel strayed away from me to worship idols must bear the consequences of their unfaithfulness" (Ezekiel 44:10, NLT).

God said that the priests of the tribe of Levi abandoned Him. They strayed away from the Lord to worship idols. They did not follow His commands, and they led the people of Israel to sin against the Lord.

The end of verse 10 says something interesting. It says that because of their detestable behavior, these priests in the tribe of Levi *"must bear the consequences of their unfaithfulness."*

What do you think those consequences should be? They should be kicked out of the Temple and stripped of their stature as priests, and they should be put to death for polluting the land of Israel with sin, right? However, this is not what happens at all. Look at verses 11 and 12.

"They may still be Temple guards and gatekeepers, and they may slaughter the animals brought for burnt offerings and be present to help the people. [12] But they encouraged my people to worship idols, causing Israel to fall into deep sin. So I have taken a solemn oath that they must bear the consequences for their sins, says the Sovereign Lord" (Ezekiel 44:11-12, NLT).

They weren't to be kicked out of the Temple at all. In fact, they were to remain in the Temple, guarding it, watching its gates, slaughtering the animals, and helping the people! If the consequences for their sin was not in being kicked out of the Temple, then what were the consequences that they were to endure? Look at verse 13.

"They may not approach me to minister as priests. They may not touch any of my holy things or the holy offerings, for they must bear the shame of all the detestable sins they have committed" (Ezekiel 44:13, NLT).

Did you catch it? Their consequence was that they could remain in the Temple but not come near the presence of God! They were not allowed any longer to touch any of His holy things, nor approach the Lord in any way. Verse 14 is a summary statement of their role moving forward.

"They are to serve as the Temple caretakers, taking charge of the maintenance work and performing general duties" (Ezekiel 44:14, NLT).

For so many churches, the glory has departed and this is all that church has become, performing maintenance work and doing general duties:

Opening the doors,

Lighting the candles,

Preparing the order of worship,

Greeting the people,

Getting the Hospitality area ready for new visitors like the associate Pastor that I talked to does every Sunday.

What's the most important part that is missing in our gatherings today? The glory and presence of God! Yet, for so many Pastors, all they are doing is performing the general and maintenance duties of the church without drawing near to the presence of God!

I was talking with a Pastor the other day that said this, *"We are asking the wrong questions. We should be asking "why" we ask all of these people to gather on Sunday mornings, Sunday evenings, and Wednesday evenings. Why are we doing what we are doing? Instead, we are asking "what." What are the numbers? What's the attendance? We're asking all the wrong questions."*

He's exactly right, yet for so many people, this is what their religion is: going through the motions, doing this, doing that, without experiencing the power and the presence of the Lord. I don't want to be a part of anything that is void and absent of the presence of God!

Notice next, the other line of priests.

"However, the Levitical priests of the family of Zadok continued to minister faithfully in the Temple when Israel abandoned me for idols. These men will serve as my ministers. They will stand in my presence and offer the fat and blood of the sacrifices, says the Sovereign Lord.

[16] *They alone will enter my sanctuary and approach my table to serve me. They will fulfill all my requirements"* (Ezekiel 44:15-16, NLT).

The Levitical Priests of the Family of Zadok ministered faithfully in the Temple when Israel abandoned God for idols, and God says about them:

They will serve as MY ministers,

They will stand in MY presence,

They will enter MY sanctuary,

They will approach MY table,

They will fulfill MY requirements,

They and they alone may serve ME.

The godly gentleman that gave me Ezekiel 44 said to me after I had read the passage, *"Matt, God has taken you from the general maintenance duties of the Temple. You are now a priest in the line of Zadok, and you are to minister unto Him."*

I was blown away. It was exactly what I needed to hear. Ezekiel 44 has quickly become my favorite passage!

Let me now ask you, *"Are you a priest in the line of the Levites, burdened with the task of performing the exhausting, menial tasks of temple maintenance without drawing near to the presence of God?"*

For so many people who drive to a building each week, this is all they encounter. No presence, and no power. They drive to the building and leave the building never changed because the entire experience has become an empty, man-made ritual!

Pastors, become a priest in the line of Zadok!

Minister unto the Lord!

Draw near to Him!

Forget about the menial tasks of the Temple!

Be released from that in Jesus' name!

Listen to the Lord and let your people go!

Let them experience the Holy Spirit in them!

Disciple them and mature them so that they can be sent out to do that with others!

Let them see that their body is the Temple of the Holy Spirit!

Let them experience the Lord's presence as they go to their neighbors!

Let them experience the Lord's presence as they gather together in community!

Let them experience the Lord's presence as they give generously and use their spiritual gift!

This is no longer a matter of performing the general maintenance duties of the temple. No! We must let go of the temple mentality and we must let go of the Old Testament understanding of Church.

God is looking for priests in the line of Zadok who will follow the Lord and who will allow the people to minster unto Him, no matter the cost!

In The Fullness of Time

When I was traveling through Asia Minor, this phrase kept coming to my mind from the book of Galatians, *"In the fullness of time."* In this passage, Paul is talking about how Jesus came at just the right time. It didn't dawn on me what exactly that meant until I traveled to the lands of the New Testament.

Alexander the Great, born in 356BC, spread Greek culture, Greek thought and the Greek language throughout the known world. Everyone that was conquered wound up speaking the Greek language. Rome had become a super-power. What did they do? They built roads throughout their Empire. If you take all of the roads that the Romans built and stretch them from end to end, they would span the globe twice.

When Jesus arrived on the scene, he arrived to Greek thought and influence and Rome at the height of its power. When Paul began preaching, he didn't have to learn the different languages of all the people. Why? They all knew Greek! His letters were written in Greek. The New Testament was written in Greek to a Greek audience. And, how did he get around? He walked on all the Roman roads!

"But how can they call on him to save them unless they believe in him? And how can they believe in him if they have never heard about him? And how can they hear about him unless someone tells them? [15] And how will anyone go and tell them without being sent? That is why the Scriptures say, 'How beautiful are the feet of messengers who bring good news!'" (Romans 10:14-15, NLT).

I had the privilege of walking some of these same roads. I was deeply impressed with the little road that made its way from Neopolis to the ancient port there along the Via Egnatia. I definitely believe the Lord is calling the Church to walk a different road, a different path by the sovereignty of His good timing.

Rather than walking a road of attraction and spending all of our efforts and energy toward that, what if God is trying to change the way we think by having us walk a completely different road, a road that is based entirely on the New Testament and the way the early Church functioned?

[1] A.W. Tozer as quoted in Christianity Today by Mark Woods, *"A.W. Tozer: 10 Quotes From A 20th Century Prophet."* (March 31, 2016). www.christianitytoday.com.

[2] Sheep Among Wolves Documentary Film, vol. 2. www.sheepamongwolvesfilm.com.

Chapter 8

WHAT HAVE WE UNINTENTIONALLY CREATED?

Thanks to COVID-19 and the *"exposure"* of the Church that it has created, we are seeing exactly what we have been reaping since Constantine. What have we unintentionally created because of our current system of doing church? What is our current system producing? Let me give you a few things.

Spectators

When I was pastoring a *"traditional"* church (Sunday morning meetings, sitting in rows, gathering at a specific place), we functioned as a mobile church. We had to set up and tear down every week. We did this for twelve of the years that I was there as Senior Pastor. Was it hard? Yep. Did it take a lot of people helping? Yep, again. Did the people struggle and sometimes complain? Yep, yep, yep!

When work needs to be done in a church that's big enough and has enough money, what usually happens? You hire what you need. When the church operates as a business, that's what you do. You hire. Part-time, full-time, $20 a week-time. If you look at church growth strategy books for this kind of system, that's what they will tell you to do.

It's called *"outsourcing,"* and it unintentionally creates these kinds of thoughts:

"We don't have to do the work, that's what the staff is there for."

"We don't have to read our Bibles. The Pastor will tell us all that we need to know."

"We don't have to teach our children Biblical truth, that's what the Children's Pastor is there for," and on and on we could go.

Sunday mornings, at any church gathering, happens to be the most segregated time on the planet, and I'm not just talking about race. I'm talking about parents and children. Parents go one way into the *"adult"* service and kid's go into their own environments. They meet up afterwards, the kids show their parents the picture that they made, and they all head home.

I saw this over and over and never thought anything about it. We had the largest children's ministry in the city, but I never thought about the unintended consequences that we were creating through this system. Parental discipleship is being outsourced to the paid people at the church building which is something that the New Testament never intended.

Years ago, I went to this church conference at one of the biggest churches in America. They had all the bells and whistles when it came to their children's ministry environments. It was hard to take it all in. However, there was one thing that I saw that I will never forget. In the midst of all of this elaborate staging and elaborate programming for kids, was this tube filled with colorful balls above the staging. Everyone in the room could see it.

The person in charge of the environment came to a quiet moment in the performance and said, *"Do you know what that tube of balls represents? It represents all the hours in a year minus 52; The one hour we spend with these kids each week for a year versus the 8,708 hours that parents spend with their kids every year."*

I thought, *"Yes! That's it! It's about parent ministry, not children's ministry. That's what we need to focus on."* Yet, how can you do that when the system that we have created is pulling us back to the one hour a week gathering at the church building?

Spiritual Infants

There might be something far worse that we are unintentionally creating in the body of Christ that is far more damaging and hurtful to the cause of Christ, and that is perpetual spiritual infancy.

The people cry, *"Feed me. Teach me."* People leave church fellowships because they are not being *"fed"* enough. One Pastor that I saw preached from a high chair in front of his congregation, kicking, whining, and screaming telling his people that this is the way they act.

I heard of another Pastor that had the hardest time getting people to volunteer in the children's ministry department. He stood on the platform and said, *"Because we did not get enough volunteers for the children's department, I'm leaving to go do that,"* and he walked off the platform. I guess his congregation didn't get the hint because he did the same thing the very next Sunday. I'm sure people volunteered after that if only to keep their preacher from spending all his time in the children's department. The people were committed to sit and listen but not serve. Are these Pastors justified in their frustration? Yes. Are they also unintentionally perpetuating the system? Yes!

The system we have created produces spiritual infants still nursing at their mother's breast.

"I can't share my faith. I don't know enough to do that."

"Disciple someone? Me? I'm still growing myself."

"Teach? I'm not the Pastor. I've never been to seminary."

Let me show you what the writer of Hebrews would say to them.

"There is much more we would like to say about this, but it is difficult to explain, especially since you are spiritually dull and don't seem to listen. [12] You have been believers so long now that you ought to be teaching others. Instead, you need someone to teach you again the basic things about God's word. You are like babies who need milk and cannot eat solid food. [13] For someone who lives on milk is still an infant and doesn't know how to do what is right. [14] Solid food is for those who are mature, who through training have the skill to recognize the difference between right and wrong" (Hebrews 5:11-14, NLT).

He calls the Church *"infants"* who live on milk! Spiritual infancy is plaguing the American Church. Instead of being spoon fed and always ingesting, we as true believers ought to be so far along in our Christian walk that we are teaching others. We ought to be so mature that we know our spiritual gifts and use them well to serve one another. We ought to be so far along in maturity that we know exactly how to do the work of ministry.

What would the Apostle Paul say to our generation today? Exactly what he said to the Corinthian believers.

"Dear brothers and sisters, when I was with you I couldn't talk to you as I would to spiritual people. I had to talk as though you belonged to this world or as though you were infants in Christ. [2] I had to feed you with milk, not with solid food, because you weren't ready for anything stronger. And you still aren't ready," (I Corinthians 3:1-2, NLT).

Once again, the words *"infant"* and *"milk"* are used to describe the believers to whom he was writing. What was the primary message from the Apostle Paul for the Corinthian believers? *"Grow to maturity."* He longed for them to be mature, but they wanted to go back to their sinful ways. What kind of letter would the Apostle Paul write to the American Church today?

Someone that I greatly respect in the faith once told me, *"Matt, do you know how long Paul left those believers and returned back to them expecting to give them meat but not being able to? Eighteen months."* A year and a half!

Paul expected complete maturing in eighteen months and yet we have seasoned believers of 30 and 40 years who say they have definitely not reached maturity! Look at what Paul tells the Colossae believers.

"He is the one we proclaim, admonishing and teaching everyone with all wisdom, so that we may present everyone fully mature in Christ. [29] *To this end I strenuously contend with all the energy Christ so powerfully works in me"* (Colossians 1:28-29, NIV).

Salvation of the people was not the end all for the Apostle Paul. He proclaimed Jesus and taught everyone about Him so that he could present everyone to Jesus as fully mature in Him. He does this with all the energy that he has. Maturity mattered to Paul. This was goal, and it must become the goal once again. Not attendance, not attraction, but maturity.

Stationary Saints

We also need to elaborate more about this idea of stationary saints. What do I mean? We have made gathering way more important than going. Read that again: We've made GATHERING way more important than GOING.

A few decades ago, *"gathering"* used to mean every Sunday morning, Sunday night and Wednesday night. Now, someone is considered to be a *"regular church attender"* if he or she attends three out of eight weekends. [1]

People are made to believe from the Pastors that stand at the front, that they need to gather at the church building every time the doors are opened. I once went to a church growth conference at a *"mega-church,"* and they were talking to us about the importance of the weekend, specifically Sunday. *"It's all about Sunday, stupid"* was the phrase. Don't plan any other church events that interfere with people gathering to the Sunday service.

It's engrained in us who grew up going to church that Sunday morning is reserved for church attendance, and if you miss for some reason, it feels out of place.

Let's talk about *"going"* for one second. Answer this question: In the last five years, how many people have come up to you and shared their faith with you as if you were lost? I'm not asking how many people you have shared your faith with in the last five years. I'm asking how many people have come up to you and shared their faith with you? When I answer that question in my own life, I cannot remember someone doing that.

I honestly believe, with the times that I've asked that question to people, we do not do a good job of sharing our faith. Instead, we would rather cloister in the confines of the *"safe"* church building and be around other Christians who are a lot like us. I get it. The fellowship is sweet, and it is a joy to be around the Body of Christ, at least most of the time!

While I was in seminary, I noticed a pattern. We were at a Christian school, surrounded by ministerial students. Many of those students worked at a church during the week which meant they were around church people all throughout the week and on Sundays.

Their whole work life, school life and social life revolved around Christians, and it seems like this is the focal point of the Church today. We want Heaven on earth (Christian neighbors, Christian schools, Christian friends, Christian jobs, Christian everything) instead of wanting to get people from earth into Heaven!

When I was younger, my Pastor gave a wonderful illustration that is now burned in my mind. He had a kerosene lantern sitting on the pulpit. When he turned it on, with all the lights on in the auditorium, you barely noticed it. Why? There was too much light. Then, he asked for all the lights to be turned off in our four-thousand seat auditorium. Only that kerosene lantern remained lit, and it burned brightly. Everyone in that auditorium got the message. The light of Jesus burns the brightest and makes the most impact, not in the light, but in the dark.

At a time when I was very young, I remember reading something that made a deep impression on me, even to this day. It was in a booklet produced by *"Our Daily Bread."* The story went like this.

"I had a dream. In my dream was an ocean full of drowning people. There was a rock that came up out of the ocean. Some people crawled up on that rock and got to safety.

As I watched, 10 percent of the people on the rock became active in making ropes and ladders, getting near the edge, trying to pull others up on the rock. But 90 percent became very active in their rock gardens, their rock music, their rock jobs, their rock lives. They had a lot of rock meetings where they spent lots of time developing their programs to go back to the ocean—but they never went.

The thought that kept coming through all the time in the dream was, 'Could they have forgotten that they themselves were once in the sea?'

A small group of people who seemed to be the leaders bothered me even more. They spent time trying to get up higher on the rock. It seemed they didn't want to get near the edge because it was risky down there. The dead, the diseased, the lost—they were down there. But the groups on the rock spent more time cloistered in false security on the higher parts of the rock. Yet every one of them heard a voice say, "Will you come? Will you help Me?" [2]

Is this where we are as the Church? Cloistered in *"safety"* away from all the *"bad"* people that we don't want our children to hang around? How did we get to this point? The Gospel is all about rescuing. It's all about going. It's all about making disciples. Jesus didn't stay in the safety of Heaven. He could have. He didn't have to save us, yet He did. Praise God for that! This must be the mindset of everyone in the Church as well.

Spectators, spiritual infants, and stationary saints do not in any way characterize what the Apostle Paul taught or expected from the believers in the New Testament, but this is exactly what our *"church factories"* are producing. This is why we must pull the plug, stop production, and align ourselves with what God wants: discipleship, maturity and going to our neighbors, the nation and the world.

[1] Rebecca Barnes, Lindy Lowry, *"7 Startling Facts: An Up Close Look at Church Attendance in America."* (January 19, 2014). www.churchleaders.com.

[2] Bill Fay, *"How Can I Share My Faith Without an Argument?"* Discovery Series: Radio Bible Class (Grand Rapids, Michigan, 1991), 30-31.

Chapter 9

CHICKEN FAITH VS PIG FAITH

Living in the deep South, you get a different perspective on a lot of things. My friend, who is a lawyer in town, told our Bible study a story that has stuck with me.

A chicken and a pig were walking down the road when they came upon a breakfast joint.

The sign out front read, "Best bacon and eggs in town."

The pig looked at the chicken and said, "Does that bother you?"

The chicken said, "No, not really, after all it only costs me a couple of eggs."

The chicken said to the pig, "Does that bother you?"

The pig replied, "Of course. For me to give anything MEANS THAT I GIVE MY LIFE."

Do you understand the connection? Most of us, if we are brutely honest, are chicken Christians.

We give a couple of eggs and go home and we feel really good about that. It doesn't really cost us much to follow Jesus, and Pastors have come to expect this and embrace this. *"Just give me a couple of eggs!"*

A guy in my Friday morning Bible study threw this out and it has bothered me ever since he said it. *"Christians are good at taking up the cause of the unborn but not the born."*

Should we be taking up the cause of the unborn? Yes, of course, but what's the cost for taking up the cause of the unborn? I mean, what does it really cost us? An opinion? A disagreement at work? A spat on social media?

But then it's over, and we move on.

What's the cost for taking up the cause of the born, those in the foster care and adoption care system? What does it cost you when you're involved in that? Your home? Your food? Your time? Your money? Your attention? Your everything? The cost is great!

What costs more, giving to missions or going on the mission field? To give to missions is a couple of eggs but to go on the mission field, that's everything.

When it comes to our churches, what's easier? Walking into a church building, sitting, listening and going home or opening up your home and inviting the messy situations of people's lives into your living room? How about inviting your neighbors over who do not know God? What about being accountable to people? See what I mean? One version of Christianity costs you a couple of eggs. The other, a whole lot more.

If you go through your life as a follower of Christ, what is it costing you to follow Jesus? Would you say that you are more of a chicken Christian or a pig Christian? In the early Church, there were only pig Christians and the ones who weren't were questioned as if maybe they weren't really Christians at all.

The Apostle Paul said that to the Corinthian church in 1 Corinthians 15.

"Think carefully about what is right, and stop sinning. For to your shame I say that some of you don't know God at all" (1 Corinthians 15:34, NLT).

Because of their lifestyle and because of their lack of maturity, the Apostle Paul said about them that he was genuinely confused as to who was really a Christ-follower and who was not. Once again, if he was writing to our generation in America today, what would he put in his letter to us? Look at Hebrews 11. It's all about pig faith.

"How much more do I need to say? It would take too long to recount the stories of the faith of Gideon, Barak, Samson, Jephthah, David, Samuel, and all the prophets. [33] By faith these people overthrew kingdoms, ruled with justice, and received what God had promised them. They shut the mouths of lions, [34] quenched the flames of fire, and escaped death by the edge of the sword. Their weakness was turned to strength. They became strong in battle and put whole armies to flight. [35] Women received their loved ones back again from death. But others were tortured, refusing to turn from God in order to be set free. They placed their hope in a better life after the resurrection. [36] Some were jeered at, and their backs were cut open with whips. Others were chained in prisons. [37] Some died by stoning, some were sawed in half, and others were killed with the sword. Some went about wearing skins of sheep and goats, destitute and oppressed and mistreated. [38] They were too good for this world, wandering over deserts and mountains, hiding in caves and holes in the ground. [39] All these people earned a good reputation because of their faith, yet none of them received all that God had promised. [40] For God had something better in mind for us, so that they would not reach perfection without us" (Hebrews 11:32-40, NLT).

And yet, hardly any of our lives look like this.

When a plague hit the region of Caesarea in the early fourth-century, the people began fleeing the city for safety in the countryside, everyone except the Christians. Eusebius, who was the bishop of the city and a historian of the early Church, wrote about them:

"All day long some of [the Christians] tended to the dying and to their burial, countless numbers with no one to care for them. Others gathered together from all parts of the city a multitude of those withered from famine and distributed bread to them all." [1]

He goes on to state that because of their compassion in the midst of the plague, the Christians' *"deeds were on everyone's lips, and they glorified the God of the Christians."* [2]

Julian, the last pagan Caesar of the Roman Empire, asked his pagan priests to imitate the love of the Christians stating,

"[They] support not only their poor, but ours as well, and all men see that our people lack aid from us." [3]

It was this witness of love that caused many people to come to Christ. Why don't many of us live like this? Let me give you a couple of reasons.

We've Changed Normal

Instead of seeing radical as normal, we've radicalized normal. When we see radical, it seems so radical because we have accepted *"un-radical"* as the normal. Do you understand that there is nothing normal about the Christian life? The normal Christian life is all about Christ living in you and unleashing Himself through you.

Look at Philippians 2.

"Though he was God, he did not think of equality with God as something to cling to. [7] Instead, he ***gave up*** *his divine privileges;* ***he took the humble position of a slave*** *and was born as a human being.*

When he appeared in human form, [8] he ***humbled himself*** *in obedience to God and* ***died*** *a criminal's death on a cross"* (Philippians 2:6-8, NLT, emphasis mine).

He gave up Heaven in order to embrace the depravity of earth.

He gave up the highest rank of Heaven in order to embrace the lowest rank on earth.

He gave up the crown in order to embrace the cross, and this is what He longs to do in us;

Give up chicken faith and embrace pig faith!

My lawyer friend that told me the chicken and pig story, set up his house as a homeless shelter. He started taking care of a mother and her children. Soon, the mother stopped coming back. He now has custody of the kids.

I told him that we were expecting to receive a foster child any day. He said, *"Most Christians don't live like this. People think I'm radical, but radical is actually Biblical."*

He's exactly right. He works with the foster care community all the time, and he told me something that made my mouth drop open. He said that Christian families will take babies but not really those in upper age. He said that they recently had to give a child over to the care of a family with two moms because in his words, "No *one else would take them."*

Let me put this in context. There are eight zillion churches on every corner in our area! Where was the Church when it was needed the most? Absent!

He went on to tell me that if you ask someone to help move a struggling family, there will be people lined up with their pick-up trucks to help. They will do whatever you need them to do, but ask them to take in a needy family or a foster child into their own homes? No one answers.

It all goes back to chicken faith versus pig faith. Helping someone move costs you a little bit of time and a little bit of gas...a couple of eggs. But, taking someone into your family, what does that cost you? A whole lot more. Most *"Christians"* only want to give a couple of eggs.

We've Idolized Safety

Dr. Paul Tournier, Swiss physician, author and pastoral counselor says, *"All of us have vast reservoirs of full potential, but the roads that lead to those reservoirs are guarded by the dragon of fear."* [4]

Remember the account between Jesus and Peter?

One day as Jesus was preaching on the shore of the Sea of Galilee, great crowds pressed in on him to listen to the word of God. [2] *He noticed two empty boats at the water's edge, for the fishermen had left them and were washing their nets.* [3] *Stepping into one of the boats, Jesus asked Simon, its owner, to push it out into the water. So he sat in the boat and taught the crowds from there.* [4] *When he had finished speaking, he said to Simon, "Now go out where it is deeper, and let down your nets to catch some fish"* (Luke 5:1-4, NLT).

God doesn't care one bit about your safety when it comes to following Him. He cares about your surrender to Him as He calls you into deeper water, and He will call you into deeper water.

What did He say to the rich, young ruler? *"Go sell everything you have and give it to the poor. Then come and follow Me."*

"But, Pastor Matt, that sounds so scary. Can you give me any assurance that things will work out okay?"

No.

But, I can give you the greatest assurance.

God promises to be with you!

What God calls you into, He will go with you!

What God initiates, He sustains!

What God prompts and starts, He supplies!

What God asks of you, He provides!

He will do everything possible to confront your safety and draw you into the deeper water where He is.

We've Embraced a False Gospel

Where in Scripture does it say, *"Raise your hand, pray a prayer and you're in?"* Where does it say that? What is the real Gospel? The Gospel is when you see your sin, when God reveals that to you, and you repent and believe in Christ, putting your trust in what He accomplished on the cross. The evidence is when He comes into your life and changes you into a new creature.

This is what the book of 1 John is all about.

"I write these things to you who believe in the name of the Son of God so that you may know that you have eternal life" (1 John 5:13, NIV).

John in essence is saying, *"If you know Christ, there will be evidence, radical evidence!"* Notice what else he says.

"We know what real love is because Jesus gave up his life for us. So we also ought to ***give up our lives*** *for our brothers and sisters. [17] If someone has enough money to live well and* ***sees a brother or sister in need*** *but shows no compassion—how can God's love be in that person?*

[18] Dear children, let's not merely say that we love each other; let us show the truth by our actions. [19] ***Our actions will show that we belong to the truth****, so we will be confident when we stand before God"* (1 John 3:16-19, NLT, emphasis mine).

This is pig faith.

Jesus gave up his position, took on the position of a slave, humbled Himself and embraced the cross. Look at what John tells the believers: Give up your lives when you see a brother or sister in need. It's the same thing!

If we don't see much of this, pig faith, then could it be that we are filling Hell with people who think they are going to Heaven but are actually not? Those who have a form of Christ but not really Him? Could it be evidenced by the fact that many of God's supposed *"people"* have never reached maturity?

John says that Christ will make Himself known in our lives, demonstrated by His radical actions as He lives in us, which should be normal in a Christian's life.

Author and speaker, Francis Chan, once gave an analogy using a balance beam as a prop.

He had everyone imagine that they were at the Olympics on the balance beam performing a routine. But, instead of doing a risk-filled routine, he imagined someone just laying down on the beam and hugging it really tightly with their arms and legs. After a while of just clinging to the beam, they carefully crawl off the beam and dismount, with their arms held high, like they've just performed an incredibly difficult routine!

If you were the judge, what kind of score would you give? What would you say if you saw someone do that for their routine during the Olympics?

"You're an Olympian?" "What was that?"

And yet, we boil our Christian life down to going to a church building on Sundays, giving a little of our money every once in a while, all the while trying to live a very comfortable life. Then we pray something like this at the end, *"God, let me die in my sleep so I won't even feel it and then I'll go up to Heaven."*

And you dismount, with your arms held high. What's God supposed to say?

If you think through your life as a follower of Christ, what is it costing you to follow Jesus?

Would you say that you are more of a chicken Christian, just a couple of eggs, or a pig Christian, it costs me everything, or not a true Christian at all? In your actions, are you more of a chicken Christian or a pig Christian or a false Christian?

In the area of rescuing the vulnerable?

In the area of getting to know your neighbors?

In the area of sharing your faith or publicly preaching?

In the area of missions and the mission field?

In the area of opening up your home?

In the area of giving up your life for the brothers and sisters in the faith?

In the area of tithing?

Then ask yourself: Have I changed normal? Have I made an idol out of safety? Have I potentially embraced a false Gospel? Dear God, deliver us from chicken faith and move us toward pig faith!

[1] Matt Crawford, *"The Compassion of Early Christians,"* (February 7, 2020). www.biblemesh.com.

[2] Ibid.

[3] Ibid.

[4] Paul Tournier, quoted in Keith Miller and Bruce Larson, *The Edge of Adventure* (Waco, TX: Word Publishing, 1976), 180.

Chapter 10

GATHERING VS GOING

What would it look like if we stopped everything that we are doing in our churches and Biblically reevaluated? What if we actually looked at the pages of the New Testament and pursued shaping our churches around that model of church? What would it cost us to do that? What would it cause us to change? What would it cause us to sacrifice?

One thing that thinking Biblically would cause us to think differently about what we consider *"valuable"* in the church.

I opened up the book of Isaiah chapter 1 the other day during my time with the Lord. I have read that chapter several times as I've read through the book of Isaiah, but don't you love how the Word of God speaks? When I read chapter 1 the other day, it was like I was reading something that I had never read before.

Listen to the Lord, you leaders of "Sodom."
Listen to the law of our God, people of "Gomorrah."
11 *"What makes you think I want all your sacrifices?"*
says the Lord.
"I am sick of your burnt offerings of rams

and the fat of fattened cattle.
I get no pleasure from the blood
of bulls and lambs and goats.
12 *When you come to worship me,*
who asked you to parade through my courts with all your ceremony?
13 *Stop bringing me your meaningless gifts;*
the incense of your offerings disgusts me!
As for your celebrations of the new moon and the Sabbath
and your special days for fasting—
they are all sinful and false.
I want no more of your pious meetings.
14 *I hate your new moon celebrations and your annual festivals.*
They are a burden to me. I cannot stand them!
15 *When you lift up your hands in prayer, I will not look.*
Though you offer many prayers, I will not listen,
for your hands are covered with the blood of innocent victims.
16 *Wash yourselves and be clean!*
Get your sins out of my sight.
Give up your evil ways.
17 *Learn to do good.*
Seek justice.
Help the oppressed.
Defend the cause of orphans.
Fight for the rights of widows" (Isaiah 1:10-17, NLT).

To whom are these words addressed? Judah. Not wayward, wicked Israel, but Judah, the line of Davidic kings, including the Messiah, the Lord Jesus Christ.

The Lord Almighty tells them, and I believe He's telling His Church today, that He does not delight in our pompous ceremony and ritual and entertainment and gathering for the sake of gathering.

"Pastor Matt, are you telling me that God doesn't want our meetings?"

Read very carefully.

If our gatherings on Sundays are nothing more than empty, man-made rules and efforts and man-made hype, then NO. If it is just checking off the list every Sunday, which is what many, many people do, then NO. If we gather without the purpose of going, then NO, NO, NO!

"Okay, then what does He want?"

Go back to Isaiah 1: Here's what He tells the people of Judah.

"Wash yourselves and be clean! Get your sins out of my sight. Give up your evil ways. [17] Learn to do good. Seek justice. Help the oppressed. Defend the cause of orphans. Fight for the rights of widows" (Isaiah 1:16-17, NLT).

Read that again. Don't miss this: *"Defend the cause of orphans. Fight for the rights of widows."*

Do these words remind you of another passage in the New Testament? It echoes James 1:27.

"Pure and genuine religion in the sight of God the Father means caring for orphans and widows in their distress and refusing to let the world corrupt you" (James 1:27, NLT).

James 1:27 is the heartbeat of the Gospel, written by the brother of Jesus. This is what *"Going"* is all about. It is going to the fatherless and the husbandless. At the time that James was writing this, if these two groups of people were left to themselves, they were reduced to begging, stealing, selling themselves, and starving.

They represent the most marginalized, disenfranchised, on the fringe, vulnerable, taken advantage of, and helpless people on the face of the earth.

James tells us that it is our responsibility to care for them in their distress. We are to care for them and visit them as Jesus cared for us and visited us.

So often we skip over the last part of this verse which says that we must refuse to let the world corrupt us, but I believe it is the most critical part of the verse.

It's the detachment from the world that allows for the attachment to the widow and the orphan.

Because of that, I believe this verse is best understood in reverse as it captures the same intended meaning of Isaiah 1. This is a summary of it.

"Don't let the world's system, thought process, and values contaminate you, so that you can free yourself up to care for the most vulnerable people on this earth in the same way that Jesus cared for us. This is the purest and most genuine religion in the sight of God."

Let me point out something in this verse. The word *"religion"* is misleading. I believe the best way to translate this word is by using the word *"worship"* in its place.

Here is the impact of what James is saying: The purest, most genuine way to worship God is to detach from the world so that you can attach to the orphan and widow.

Think about this from God's perspective. God is saying through this verse and in Isaiah 1, *"This is how I want you to worship Me above all else. This is what I supremely desire. This is for what My heart beats most. This is what supremely pleases Me the most, to care for the orphan and the widow."*

And we say, *"God, I will sing to You and raise my hands to You once a week."* It is no wonder that God no longer wants our worship, as stated in Isaiah 1, if it is offered while neglecting the orphan and widow. As a matter of fact, He says that this kind of *"worship"* makes Him sick, giving Him no pleasure or delight. He says to stop, that it disgusts Him, and that it is considered to Him as sinful and false. He wants no more of it. He hates it, can't stand it, and it is a burden to Him. He will not look at it or even listen to it.

There are 153 million orphans in the world as I write these words.

Let that sink in.

In the U.S., there are 400,000 children in the foster care system and 100,000 of those are available for adoption right now.

How many church bodies are there presently in the U.S.? Around 300,000. Even if one church body collectively cared for one child in foster care, we could make a huge dent in the foster care system. And, yet we don't!

Why? Why? Why? I'm sure there are multiple reasons like fear or just being unaware, but I want to focus on two specific reasons:

We've Been Polluted By The World

What does James mean by *"world"* here? It is the total system of evil that is in opposition to God and His righteous ways. It is the system of the world that exalts MONEY, POWER, PLEASURE.

When we look at the orphan crisis, we speak about it from the world's perspective. We say things like,

"I can't adopt or foster a child, I can barely take care of myself."

"I have to look out for my 401k."

"I just retired."

"I want to travel."

"I have my own family to take care of."

And on and on we go. It's all just a way to say, *"I've adopted the world's value system."*

The Apostle John in 1 John says it like this: *"Do not love the world or the things in the world..."*

God broke me a few weeks ago. Broke me. I heard a sermon about weeping. *"What do you weep for?"* So, I asked God to make me weep. *"Bring weeping into my life this week."* I was watching a video that my brother sent me about this girl who had been abused in a bad home environment. She had run away to the streets when she was 11 years old and started making a living by selling her body. I lost it. One of my daughters was 11 at the time.

I put my hands in my face and wept. The thought that kept coming to me was this, *"Every child deserves a good home"* and *"Every child needs to be protected and loved by a good dad."*

Everything that I valued up until that point (a bigger house, sports cars, material things of this world) were gone. I told myself and the Lord that if rescuing children meant me sleeping on the back porch and driving a beat-up pick-up truck for the rest of my life then I would relish that opportunity with joy.

I don't want to be polluted by the world any longer. When God brings you to a point where you refuse to let the world corrupt you, this is where God puts your eyes, on the orphan and the widow, because this is the closest thing to the heart of the Father.

Why else don't we run after the orphan and the widow?

We've Made An Idol Out of Worship

Remember Isaiah 1? *"Who asked you to parade through My courts...? I want no more of your pious meetings."* They had made an idol out of worship and ceremony, thinking that is what God wanted, and we've done the same thing.

We've said, *"Look God, I'm showing up for an hour with my family. I'm even raising my hands to You in worship every week."* But, if that's all it is, then He doesn't want it.

Have you ever told somebody what to get you for a present? They asked you, maybe for your birthday or Christmas, and you told them? What if instead of getting you what you asked for, they bought you something else, something totally different? Let me ask you, *"When you open the present, would you be happy? Would you be disappointed? Would you be confused?"*

Folks, this is what God is asking for, begging for. *"Worship Me in this way. Detach yourself from the world, so that you can attach yourself to the orphan and widow and care for them."*

The meaning of *"caring for"* in Isaiah 1 and James 1 is the idea of *"assuming responsibility for, and giving them the means of support."* It's not a pop-in visit or a social call. It's life.

The question is,

"Will we choose to worship the Lord in the way that He most desires to be worshipped?"

Let me finish with this story. Go back to that turbulent ocean that we referenced a couple of chapters back. Imagine a big ship in the midst of that turbulent ocean. Remember, in the ocean are drowning people (the lost, the orphaned, those without hope) desperately needing to be rescued. Everyone on board the ship are people who have been at one time rescued from the water. Jesus is also on this ship. He's the Captain.

In the current model of Church that exists in America today, here's what will you find taking place on that vessel. Instead of saved people making every effort to rescue lost and perishing people in the water, you find them doing a number of things.

Sitting at the Feet of Jesus

Many long to sit at the feet of Jesus, worshipping Him at every moment. *"Oh, Jesus, You are so good. You are so great and awesome. Thank you for rescuing us. I just want to sit here at Your feet, and give You the worship that You deserve."*

"Pastor Matt, what's wrong with that?"

If you stand back and look at the whole picture of Jesus aboard this ship, you will see Him constantly pointing toward the ocean. You will find Him saying over and over, *"Go! Go get them! Go rescue them! Go help them! Go and make disciples!"*

Therefore, our *"worship"* of Him no longer looks like a good and spiritual thing. It looks more a distraction compared to what He is calling us to do which is to go back into the water and rescue sinful, dirty, vulnerable, and marginalized people who are living with no hope.

Can I tell you something?

Sitting at the feet of Jesus in worship is treasonous and disobedient as long as it neglects the mandate to GO.

Jesus has said, *"Go,"* and yet we have stayed.

Making the Ship Look Attractive

We've spent much of our financial resources on making the ship look so beautiful because our Lord is on board. We've made it so attractive thinking that possibly the people in the water would see it and be drawn to it. We've desperately tried to attract them with gimmicks and give-aways when they really need to see the Gospel and the good works of Jesus in our lives!

We've focused so much of our attention and resources on making the building as beautiful as we can, to the neglect of rescuing the perishing! Is this not true, Pastor? To test this, hold two meetings among your church body at the same time. The first meeting will be about sharing your faith and discipleship. The second meeting will be about changing the carpet, paint and pews in the sanctuary, with a vote right after. Which meeting will draw the biggest crowd?

Majored On the Minor

We've practiced our instruments and ironed our choir robes so that we can make the music on the ship pleasing to the Lord, yet what the Lord wants is for us to make disciples. Think about it, the majority of effort that is focused in the church body is focused on making the Sunday morning service as good as possible. Isn't that right? This is when *"lost"* people may wander into the service.

"Stay and come to us," is the very opposite of "GO and Make Disciples" which is what the Lord has said for us to do.

We also yell out, *"Clean up before you come in."* I've seen this over and over in many churches. I was talking to a couple who started inviting people into their home for a Bible study. They had two same-sex couples coming to the Bible study, and they had others who were clearly lost, all ready and open to know and study the Word of God! Yet, as soon as it began it stopped. The wife got offended by one of the non-Christian people coming to the study, and said that no one could come back to her home. Just like that, it was over, and the devil received the victory.

The people in the water are dirty and sinful. They have sinful lifestyles. They have outwardly sinful children. They are not going to look like us, but we must love them until they look like Jesus. We have to keep reminding ourselves that we too were once in the water. Perhaps this is what the woman in the home Bible study forgot.

We Plan on Going but Never Do

Have you ever seen a good movie? Have you ever been to a really good restaurant? With how many people did you share that experience? How many people did you tell? Let me ask you this: Did you have to take a course on *"How to Explain the Good Things that You Experience in Life to Others?"* Did you have to practice over and over what you were going to say about the food or the movie? No! Out of the overflow of your joy in that experience, you shared that joy with others.

Imagine telling your child to clean his room, but when you come back two hours later, you notice that nothing has been done. His reason?

"Dad, I've been researching all this time what "clean your room" means. I've looked up 'clean' in the Greek to see what it actually means. I've looked online at other people who have kept their rooms clean. I'm working really hard to figure out exactly what you mean."

If this was an actual conversation, what kind of look would you give him after his explanation? I believe God is giving many of us that very same look. *"Just go! Don't try to figure out what it means. Just go! Just do it! Just share Me with others, everywhere you go, out of the overflow of the joy that I have given you."*

What if every believer on the ship saw Jesus pointing into the water and obeyed? What if we started making ropes? What if we jumped into the water and shared with them the Good News of rescue? What if we impacted those who were poor, hurting, vulnerable, naked? What if that drew the attention of everyone in the water? Rescue at that point would not be viewed as judgmental but as radical love and sacrifice, the same way Jesus sacrificed for us.

What if we came upon board, tired and exhausted, and sat at Jesus' feet and said, *"Lord, I got another one?"* What would He say? *"Well done My good and faithful servant."* His encouragement would be the motivation to go out again, knowing that we are giving Jesus the worship that He truly desires.

What if our fellowship was sweetened because we were working, arm and arm, diligently obeying the Master's command? The true way to worship Jesus is in GOING! It's what He wants and most desires, and what worship should look like is coming back to the feet of Jesus in exhaustion and joy saying to Him, *"Lord, I rescued another."*

It's not about GATHERING on Sunday morning. It's all about GOING, and it starts first with the orphan and the widow. Here's what I want you to do. First, type into your phone or computer *"Foster Care"* and type in your state. See what your state says about how to start that process. Then, I want you to pray, and I want you to ask the Lord to make you weep.

Next, if you are a Pastor reading this, how can you get your people going rather than sitting? How can you get your people out of a gathering mentality and into a going mentality? Don't skip over these questions. It starts with you. Bring them before the Lord and honestly ask Him what he wants you to do.

Lastly, I want you to ask the Lord to show you if the love of the world is in you. I want you also to ask Him to convince you that what I'm sharing with you is the way that He desires to be worshipped.

Remember the impact of Isaiah 1 and James 1:27:

"Don't let the world's system, thought process, and values contaminate you, so that you can free yourself up to care for the most vulnerable people on this earth in the same way that Jesus cared for us. This is the purest and most genuine way to worship God."

God doesn't want our gathering if it neglects the mandate to GO.

Chapter 11

THE ROLE OF THE CALLED

Let's look forward to what the Church could become if we could only get back to obeying the New Testament.

When I was at my former church, we met in a high school gym. Every Sunday we had to roll out giant mats to cover the entire gym floor to prevent damage from people walking on it, and every Sunday, at the end of the service, we had to roll up those mats. I was usually there at the end of the service, helping in some way to roll them up and get them back on the cart. One Sunday, as we were rolling the floor up, I asked a young man who was standing there, whose dad is a Pastor, to help me do something, and he said, *"That's what we pay you for."*

I looked at him, thinking that he must be joking, but he didn't crack a smile. I asked him if he was serious, and he assured me that he was not kidding. In essence he was saying, *"We pay you to do the work,"* and he meant it. I was stunned because that's not what the New Testament says at all, but perhaps that's the message that we are unintentionally conveying to the Church body today. *"We pay you, Pastor. You do the work."*

If you ask any small church congregation Pastor what his role is, he will tell you that he has lots of roles:

Preaching,

Visiting the sick,

Printing the bulletin,

Handling the church budget,

Dropping off the money to the bank,

Planning the order of worship,

Attending all of the committee meetings and deacon's meetings,

Making administrative decisions for the church, along with a thousand other things.

No one has that many spiritual gifts to do all of that, yet that's what he's expected to do. It's no wonder that many Pastors that I know have experienced some sort of burnout.

A Fox News article that I read recently had this to say about Pastor burnout, *"A study of Protestant pastors conducted in March by the faith-based research organization Barna Group suggested that unprecedented numbers are thinking about quitting the ministry. The poll showed that rates of burnout among pastors have risen dramatically during the past year, with a staggering 42% of ministers wondering if they should abandon their vocation altogether. Such pastors named stress (56%), loneliness (43%), and political divisions (38%) as the top reasons they have wearied of the job, as well as the toll it has taken on their families (29%)."* [1]

I love Pastors and I love their heart for ministry, but they are carrying a load they were never intended to carry, which I believe COVID-19 has clearly shown. Not only is this mindset unbiblical, but it is also burdensome as shown with the staggering number of Pastors thinking about calling it quits.

What would it look like if our PEOPLE were actually empowered to do ministry? What would it do for our people if we actually led them to a Biblical understanding of the Church? Turn your attention to Ephesians 4.

"Now these are the gifts Christ gave to the church: the apostles, the prophets, the evangelists, and the pastors and teachers" (Ephesians 4:11, NLT).

Notice that these gifts that Jesus gave to the Church are positions of leadership within the church body. These are *"called"* positions by God.

When I was 11 years old, God called me to preach. I didn't ask for it, nor did I volunteer for it. I had other plans at age 11, primarily playing Major League Baseball, but God called me with five words, *"I want you to preach,"* and here I am.

Let me briefly describe each of these called positions of leadership.

Apostles—Those who are sent forth to expand the Kingdom.

Prophets—Those who are the *"forth-tellers"* of God's truth with an unwavering conviction.

Evangelists—Those who explain well the Good News of salvation.

Pastors—Those who shepherd the body and watch out for falsehood of any kind.

Teachers—Those who expound on and make sense of the Word of God.

Now, we try to attribute all of these gifts to one person—the Pastor, but notice that there are several called positions that Jesus gave to His Church, and for the Church to function in its fullest capacity, all of these positions must be operational.

Who gave the gifts? Christ Jesus the Lord did, and all of them are valuable and essential for the Kingdom of God. Notice what it says next:

"Their responsibility is to equip God's people to do his work and build up the church, the body of Christ" (Ephesians 4:12, NLT).

The text doesn't say that these leaders are to do the work, but that would make sense if it did. I mean, those who are good at what they do should do the majority of the work, right? But, that's not what the text says. The text clearly says that their responsibility is to equip God's people to do the work. In other words, they are to pour into the body and help the body do what the *"called"* does. This is a reversal of the arrows for sure.

But this is not what happens today in our churches, is it? What happens most often in our churches is that the people sitting in the rows sit back and watch the called perform or do the work, and we marvel at their giftedness.

As Pastors and leaders, we rise up to these expectations, to the applause of people, often working to the point of exhaustion acting like we have all of these gifts. Isn't that right? But that's not right, Biblically speaking. The text clearly says that the responsibility of the called is to equip.

My friend told me about a conversation that took place between a man in the church and the Pastor of the church. This *"layman,"* (once again an idea that is never mentioned in the Bible) shared the Gospel with someone, led him to Christ and baptized him in his bathtub. When he told the Pastor what he had done, the Pastor said that what he did was not legitimate! It was his job, and his job only, to baptize the people, even though this goes against everything in the New Testament! Can you believe that? Pastors, with all due respect, I think many of us are getting in the way, actually being a stumbling block, concerning what God wants to accomplish through His people, His royal priesthood!

What does equipping look like? It is the undertaking of completely teaching the people how to do the work of ministry.

It's not *"Read the Bible"* but *"Let us show you how to read your Bible."*

It's not *"Share your faith."* It's *"Let us teach you how to share your faith."*

It's not *"Do what's right."* It's *"Let us show you how to do what's right."*

It's not *"Serve"* but *"Let us help you know how to find your spiritual gift,"* and it's all done in the context of accountability.

Equipping is done by teaching the body how to do the work of ministry, and holding each other accountable so that the work of the church can be done by the people, not the leaders.

Please tell me, do you know of any traditional churches that do this well, fulfilling the instructions of Ephesians 4? Do you see anyone doing this within the current system that we have built? Do you see it happening as people sit in rows in these massive auditoriums (I grew up in the context of a massive auditorium), listening to someone speak and then going home? Do you see Ephesians 4 taking place in church bodies where the called equip the people to do the work of ministry, are held accountable and sent out to minister in Jesus' name?

This *"work of ministry"* is not changing diapers in the nursery. Ephesians 4 is not about being a greeter at the door of the church, or being a member of the choir. This is about doing the work of an apostle, a prophet, an evangelist, a pastor, a teacher.

When I was in Corinth, we saw some of the things that had been excavated from the site. What stood out to me was all the body parts they had found. These were not literal body parts but hand-crafted body parts used as medical examples to show all sorts of things that can go wrong with the human body: gender defects, deformities with the feet and hands. It was a little bit overwhelming. They were everywhere.

It is no wonder that Paul talked about body parts to the Corinthian church in order to explain spiritual gifts. As soon as he mentioned it to the believers in Corinth, they would have immediately connected the dots.

"Now, dear brothers and sisters, regarding your question about the special abilities the Spirit gives us. I don't want you to misunderstand this. [2] You know that when you were still pagans, you were led astray and swept along in worshiping speechless idols. [3] So I want you to know that no one speaking by the Spirit of God will curse Jesus, and no one can say Jesus is Lord, except by the Holy Spirit.

[4] There are different kinds of spiritual gifts, but the same Spirit is the source of them all. [5] There are different kinds of service, but we serve the same Lord. [6] God works in different ways, but it is the same God who does the work in all of us.

[7] A spiritual gift is given to each of us so we can help each other. [8] To one person the Spirit gives the ability to give wise advice; to another the same Spirit gives a message of special knowledge. [9] The same Spirit gives great faith to another, and to someone else the one Spirit gives the gift of healing. [10] He gives one person the power to perform miracles, and another the ability to prophesy. He gives someone else the ability to discern whether a message is from the Spirit of God or from another spirit. Still another person is given the ability to speak in unknown languages, while another is given the ability to interpret what is being said. [11] It is the one and only Spirit who distributes all these gifts. He alone decides which gift each person should have" (1 Corinthians 12:1-11, NLT).

The gifts all come from the same Spirit, and He gives gifts to everyone that He indwells. He gives the gifts that He chooses for that person to have, and He alone is the source of all the gifts. All of these gifts are for the help of others, and here's what they demonstrate: Individuals coming together to make one body. Notice what Paul says next to drive this point home.

"The human body has many parts, but the many parts make up one whole body. So it is with the body of Christ. [13] Some of us are Jews, some are Gentiles, some are slaves, and some are free. But we have all

been baptized into one body by one Spirit, and we all share the same Spirit.

14 Yes, the body has many different parts, not just one part. 15 If the foot says, "I am not a part of the body because I am not a hand," that does not make it any less a part of the body. 16 And if the ear says, "I am not part of the body because I am not an eye," would that make it any less a part of the body? 17 If the whole body were an eye, how would you hear? Or if your whole body were an ear, how would you smell anything?

18 But our bodies have many parts, and God has put each part just where he wants it. 19 How strange a body would be if it had only one part! 20 Yes, there are many parts, but only one body. 21 The eye can never say to the hand, "I don't need you." The head can't say to the feet, "I don't need you."

22 In fact, some parts of the body that seem weakest and least important are actually the most necessary. 23 And the parts we regard as less honorable are those we clothe with the greatest care. So we carefully protect those parts that should not be seen, 24 while the more honorable parts do not require this special care. So God has put the body together such that extra honor and care are given to those parts that have less dignity. 25 This makes for harmony among the members, so that all the members care for each other. 26 If one part suffers, all the parts suffer with it, and if one part is honored, all the parts are glad. 27 All of you together are Christ's body, and each of you is a part of it" (1 Corinthians 12:12-27, NLT).

Paul says that the human body and the body of Christ are exactly the same (or should be). Could you imagine one foot wanting to walk at a different pace or in a different direction from the other foot? It would be maddening to experience but funny to watch!

Just as the human body works together as ONE BODY, so everyone who has been gifted by the Holy Spirit is to come together and function as ONE BODY.

What should it look like when the body of Christ is working correctly? Everyone functioning in their spiritual gift for the blessing and benefit of others. Just as the Holy Spirit distributes gifts to individuals, when individuals minister in community they should demonstrate the full and complete picture of Jesus.

When you don't know your spiritual gift or operate in your spiritual gift, you rob the body. You make it incomplete. You make it inefficient and not work correctly. This is why we cannot exalt other gifts above the others as more important. Did you read that?

No other gift in the body of Christ is more important than the others, just like no other body part is more important than all of the others.

Every part on my body is essential as far as I'm concerned, and if the Holy Spirit gave you a gift, consider it to be very important to the rest of the body. Where is the best place for the demonstration of this spiritual gift? It is in the context of a small group of people able to fit in a home.

This is why the New Testament was birthed into a micro-context, not a macro-context. This is why God caused the Church to scatter. This is why God caused persecution to come upon the Church. It was so the Church could remain in a small context so that genuine community, maturity and discipleship could take place.

Notice what happens when the body is released and empowered in this way.

"He makes the whole body fit together perfectly. As each part does its own special work, it helps the other parts grow, so that the whole body is healthy and growing and full of love" (Ephesians 4:16, NLT).

Jesus makes the whole body fit together perfectly. Everyone operating in their spiritual gifting makes it a whole body, not lacking in any way. Paul describes exactly what a complete, physical body is supposed to do. It is to be healthy, growing and full of love. This should be the mantra of every body of believers.

The American Church is not healthy right now. When the called do the work and the people sit back and watch, it is an indictment on both sides. The strategy of the Church has to change into a strategy of accountability and equipping the body to do the work of ministry.

Pastor, read carefully. In light of the statistics that we looked at in the beginning of the book, you should quit. Not the ministry but trying to do it all by yourself. The New Testament is clear about church leadership which involves everyone in the Church, and I believe the Lord is saying to every one of His shepherds,

"LET MY PEOPLE GO! Equip them and send them out! Teach them how to evangelize. Teach them how to make disciples. Teach them how to baptize and minister in Jesus' name, and teach them how to do the work of ministry."

This is exactly what Ephesians 4 is telling us to do. The arrows have to be reversed in order for the culture to change! When that happens, I believe we will become like the New Testament Church.

Let me close with a story.

There was an American Pastor who went to China to train 22 Chinese believers. These believers rode a train for 13 hours to get to where he was. They sat on a hardwood floor in a 700 square foot apartment with no air conditioning for three days, from 8 in the morning until 5 at night hearing from the Word of God.

This Pastor asked them when they arrived, *"How many people do you 22 oversee? How many believers are under you?"* Do you know what they said? *"A little over 20 million people."* Not twenty thousand. 20 million!

When this Pastor asked them, *"How can I pray for you?"*, they said, *"In your country, you can gather whenever you want. Pray that we can gather together whenever we want and become just like you."*

Do you know what he told them? *"No. I will not pray for that."*

They said, *"Why?"*

Here's what he told them.

"Because you guys rode a train for 13 hours to get here. In my country, if you have to drive for more than an hour, people don't come.

You sat on a wooden floor for 3 days. In my country, if people have to sit for more than 45 minutes, they leave.

You sat not only here on a hard wood floor, you did it without air-conditioning. In my country, if it's not padded pews and air-conditioned, people won't often come back.

In my country we have an average of two Bibles per family. We don't read any of them. You hardly have any Bibles and you memorize them from pieces of paper.

I will not pray that you will become like us, but I will pray that we become just like you." [2]

Think about this. These 22 leaders gathered as representatives of *"a little over 20 million people."* Two things stand out to me about this:

1. *Could you even get 22 U.S. Pastors from the same city to gather together?*

2. *If they all combined their attendance numbers, would it be anywhere near 20 million people?*

Our system is failing us because we are not equipping our people, holding them accountable and releasing them in Jesus' Name!

In 1982, do you know how many estimated Christians existed in China? Three million. In 2018, do you know how many estimated Christians were believed to be in China? 80 million! In 40 years, 77 million believers were added to the Kingdom of God. That is rapid growth, even faster than what was experienced in the New Testament.

What do you know about Christians and Communist China? Christians are persecuted, imprisoned, abducted, and murdered for their faith in Christ. They are forced to worship in homes and in secret, unable to make a sound, yet the Gospel is flourishing and people are coming to Christ at a rapid rate!

This is what God wants to do among us in the West, but it's going to take us obeying Ephesians 4. Both sides. The called equipping the people to do the work of ministry and the people, the Priesthood of Believers, the Saints of God, the Priests of God being held accountable and actually doing the work of ministry.

When ministry happens like this, we will see the Church be unleashed to its full potential, displaying the full stature of Christ. Until that happens, the Church in America will continue to decline and lose its influence.

[1] Jon Brown, *"Pastors battle skyrocketing burnout amid politics, pandemic: Wearing on the soul."* (September 8, 2022). www.foxnews.com.

[2] Caleb Parker, *"Chinese Christians Jailed for Faith, Memorize Bible Because Guards 'Can't Take What's Hidden in Your Heart'."* (June 17, 2019). www.foxnews.com.

Chapter 12

GOD IN US

Let me paint a clear picture for you between the Church as we know it in our generation and the Church as it was when it first started. What do we have in the Western Church in terms of resources at our disposal and at our fingertips?

Do we have nice buildings to meet in?

Do we have the freedom to worship when we want without fear of persecution?

Do we have dozens of translations of God's Word in print and on our smart devices?

Do we have professional clergy and pastors to help us and teach us?

Do we have training facilities and seminaries to train us how to lead God's people?

Do we have commentaries and books to help us understand God's Word?

Do we have radio programs and internet sites that enhance the proclamation of God's Word?

Do we have music outlets that let us listen to worship music 24 hours a day?

Let me ask you, where as a Church are we lacking in any way when it comes to resources available to us? Nowhere. Let's contrast this with the early Church, and when I refer to the *"Early Church"* I mean from the time of Pentecost to the time just before Constantine took the throne as Roman Emperor. What resources were available to them?

Did they have nice buildings to meet in? No.

Did they have religious liberty? Of course not. They spent their time meeting in secret. There was no public, visible witness of the early Church. There were only the people who called themselves *"Followers of the Way."*

Did they have God's Word? Not in full. The New Testament wasn't canonized until after the reign of Constantine. You did have Paul's letters and the letters of the New Testament, but they were sent to certain regions of the Roman Empire like Galatia or Macedonia or Asia and circulated there.

What you really had was Paul traveling around to various parts of the Roman Empire, preaching the Good News about Christ, first to the Jew and then to the Gentile. When people believed this message, a church body was started.

Then, because an angry mob was usually on the trail of the Apostle Paul, he left town in a hurry. His second and third missionary journeys consisted of visiting those churches, seeing how they were doing and strengthening them.

Did they have professional, paid clergy to help them during this time? No.

Did they have seminaries to teach them and train them on how to lead a church body? No.

Did they have youth Pastors and children's Pastors? No.

Did they have commentaries and the tons of resources like we have today? No.

Did they have volumes of books on church growth and church strategy? No.

Scholars agree that there were about 20 to 25 thousand believers at the beginning of the Church because of the resurrection of Jesus and the coming of the Holy Spirit at Pentecost. By the time of Constantine, around 310 to 330AD, they had grown to over 20 million people. [1]

Do you understand the magnitude of that statistic? How was the early Church able to grow as rapidly as it did without all of the resources that we have today? Think about it.

They did not have radio.

They did not have TV.

They did not have internet and smart devices.

Instead of focusing on everything that they didn't have, let's understand the ONE thing that they did have, and it's the ONE thing that is the essential ingredient for every follower of Christ. Do you know what they had? They had the Holy Spirit.

Who is the Holy Spirit?

He is the third person of the Triune God (God the Father, God the Son, and God the Holy Spirit).

He is just as much God as the Father and the Son—He is no less and fully equal. He is never referred to as an *"it"* in the Bible. He is always referred to in the masculine sense, and upon salvation, God the Holy

Spirit comes to live INSIDE that person. God's Spirit comes to live inside our physical body.

If you are a *"true"* Christian, you have the Holy Spirit living IN you. This is why I continue to say that not everyone who says they are a Christian is a Christian. Christianity is not about subscribing to a certain set of rules or beliefs. *"I believe this, this and this, therefore, I am a Christian."* No, the difference between those who are and those who are not is the Holy Spirit living on the inside. Let me give you a few verses to show you what I mean.

Jesus says in John 14, regarding the Holy Spirit:

"If you love me, obey my commandments. [16] And I will ask the Father, and he will give you another Advocate, who will never leave you. [17] He is the Holy Spirit, who leads into all truth. The world cannot receive him, because it isn't looking for him and doesn't recognize him. But you know him, because he lives with you now and later will be ***in*** *you"* (John 14:15-17, NLT, emphasis mine).

Anytime I am witnessing to a Jehovah's Witness, I use their Bible to show them this verse along with several others. Why? Because they don't believe that the Holy Spirit comes to live on the inside of them. They believe that the Holy Spirit is the divine force or radiance of God that comes upon them, but not inside them. And when I show them this verse, many times, their eyes are opened and their mouths are silenced, and I simply say to them, *"If you are wrong about the Holy Spirit, perhaps you are wrong about who Jesus is as well."*

Look at these other Scriptures.

"Don't you realize that your body is the temple of the Holy Spirit, who lives ***in*** *you and was given to you by God? You do not belong to yourself,"* (1 Corinthians 6:19, NLT).

"And God has given us his Spirit as proof that we live in him and he ***in*** *us"* (1 John 4:13, NLT, emphasis mine).

"It is God who enables us, along with you, to stand firm for Christ.

He has commissioned us, [22] and he has identified us ***as his own by placing the Holy Spirit in our hearts*** *as the first installment that guarantees everything he has promised us"* (2 Corinthians 1:21-22, NLT, emphasis mine).

The Holy Spirit is the third person of the Trinity, and He promises to take up residence in your life upon belief and trust in the truth of the Gospel, but I want to show you some Scriptures that maybe you have overlooked that give us an even clearer understanding of who the Holy Spirit is. The name *"Holy Spirit"* is often interchangeable with the name *"Jesus"* or the *"Spirit of Jesus."* Let me show you.

And because we are his children, God has sent the ***Spirit of his Son into our hearts****, prompting us to call out, "Abba, Father"* (Galatians 4:6, NLT, emphasis mine).

In 2 Corinthians the Holy Spirit has been placed in our hearts. Here in Galatians, it says that the Spirit of His Son has been placed in our hearts. I love what the Apostle Paul says about himself in Galatians chapter 2.

"My old self has been crucified with Christ. It is no longer I who live, but ***Christ lives in me****. So I live in this earthly body by trusting in the Son of God, who loved me and gave himself for me"* Galatians 2:20, NLT, emphasis mine).

"For God wanted them to know that the riches and glory of Christ are for you Gentiles, too. And this is the secret: ***Christ lives in you****. This gives you assurance of sharing his glory. [28] So we tell others about Christ, warning everyone and teaching everyone with all the wisdom God has given us. We want to present them to God, perfect in their relationship to Christ. [29] That's why I work and struggle so hard, depending on* ***Christ's mighty power that works within me"*** (Colossians 1:27-29, NLT, emphasis mine).

One of the main verses that I give to Jehovah's Witnesses when talking about the Holy Spirit, who is the person of Christ living on the inside, is found in Romans 8.

*"But you are not controlled by your sinful nature. You are controlled by the Spirit if you have the Spirit of God living **in** you. (And remember that those who do not have the **Spirit of Christ** living **in** them do not belong to him at all.) [10] And **Christ lives within you**, so even though your body will die because of sin, the Spirit gives you life because you have been made right with God. [11] **The Spirit of God**, who raised Jesus from the dead, lives **in** you. And just as God raised Christ Jesus from the dead, he will give life to your mortal bodies by this same Spirit living **within** you"* (Romans 8:9-11, NLT, emphasis mine).

The testimony of Scripture is that the Holy Spirit comes to live inside a person's life. That same Spirit is also called *"The Spirit of Christ," "The Spirit of God,"* and Christ Himself. Here's what I want you to understand about the Holy Spirit that was relevant for the early Church back then and that is a must for our generation to understand today, and that is this:

The Holy Spirit is our personal Jesus

Do you remember in the book of Acts what Followers of the Way were called? It was actually a slang term meant to make fun of them. *"Christian,"* which means *"Little Christs."* What makes that *"slang"* statement so true is that if we are true followers of God, we are *"Little Christs"* because we have Jesus Christ the Lord living in all of His power and in all of His glory and in all of His person IN us.

"But we have this treasure in jars of clay to show that this all-surpassing power is from God and not from us" (2 Corinthians 4:7, NIV).

Based on this fact and understanding that Jesus has been resurrected from the dead and is alive at this very moment, let me ask you:

Was Jesus Christ a real person?

Did He walk around on this earth?

Did He have emotions?

Did He get angry?

Did He weep?

Did He care for people?

Did He love to do the Father's will?

Will He not also, if He is ungrieved and unstifled, be Himself in everything He is, in our hearts and lives as well?

This is why the Apostle Paul could honestly say, *"I no longer live. It is Christ who lives in me."*

Did Jesus speak while on this earth?

Did He heal?

Did He instruct His disciples?

Did He teach? YES!

Will He not also, if He is ungrieved and unstifled, do the same thing in our lives? If He's living on the inside, won't He make Himself known?

When I share Jesus with people, I always talk about the Holy Spirit. I tell them that the Holy Spirit comes to live and take up residence in every person that trusts in Jesus. I then say something like this to each person,

"Let me ask you two questions. If the God of the universe, who spoke this world into existence promises to live inside a person's life, would that person know it when it happened, and would that person be different?"

I shared this recently with about 25 pastors in Haiti. Every time I ask it, no matter in what culture, the answer is always the same. *"Of course!"*

Don't you get it? This is on whom the early Church relied. Jesus! They relied on Him for every single thing as Head of the Church. Let me give you some verses to show you exactly what the Holy Spirit does for us as He indwells us. Again, notice how active He is.

"If you love me, obey my commandments. [16] And I will ask the Father, and he will give you another Advocate, ***who will never leave you****.*
[17] He is the Holy Spirit, ***who leads into all truth"*** (John 14:15-17, NLT, emphasis mine).

He will be our advocate,

He will never leave,

He will lead into all truth.

You never have to fear believing a lie or being eternally deceived by erroneous doctrine because the Holy Spirit in us leads into all truth.

"But when the Father sends the Advocate as my representative—that is, the Holy Spirit—he will ***teach you everything*** *and will* ***remind you of everything I have told you"*** (John 14:26, NLT, emphasis mine).

"But you have received the Holy Spirit, and he lives within you, so you don't need anyone to teach you what is true. For the Spirit teaches you everything you need to know, and what he teaches is true—it is not a lie. So just as he has taught you, remain in fellowship with Christ" (1 John 2:27, NLT).

The Holy Spirit leads,

The Holy Spirit teaches us everything about Jesus,

The Holy Spirit reminds us of everything that Jesus has said.

Look next at what Peter tells the early Christians. Don't miss this.

"By his divine power, God has given us everything we need for living a godly life. We have received all of this by coming to know him, the one who called us to himself by means of his marvelous glory and excellence" (2 Peter 1:3, NLT).

How much has God given to us in order for us to live a godly life? Did you catch that? God has given us everything we need for living a Godly life. EVERYTHING WE NEED! How is that possible? It is possible because the Holy Spirit brings with Himself, power. Power!

Look at Acts 1 regarding *"power."*

"But you will receive power when the Holy Spirit comes upon you. And you will be my witnesses, telling people about me everywhere—in Jerusalem, throughout Judea, in Samaria, and to the ends of the earth" (Acts 1:8, NLT).

When Jesus was speaking to His disciples before ascending to Heaven, He said that when the Holy Spirit comes, they will receive power. Dynamite! What was that power going to cause them to do? To witness. To tell about life changing message concerning Christ, and to make disciples. So, the Holy Spirit gives us power to do the Father's will in every way. Look lastly at Galatians 5.

"But the Holy Spirit produces this kind of fruit in our lives: love, joy, peace, patience, kindness, goodness, faithfulness, [23] gentleness, and self-control. There is no law against these things" (Galatians 5:22-23, NLT).

The fruit of the Spirit is the nature and life of Jesus coming out in us. Who produces the fruit? The Holy Spirit produces the fruit of Jesus in our lives. It is not us exhibiting these characteristics in our own power. Don't miss this. It is the Holy Spirit producing this in us who have Him living on the inside. Understand once again,

The Holy Spirit never leaves,

He leads into all Truth,

He teaches us everything about Jesus and brings to memory everything Jesus has said,

He gives us everything we need for living a godly life,

He gives us His power to do the Father's will in every way,

He produces the character and life of Jesus in us, the fruit of the Spirit, and so much more.

It is Jesus Christ the Lord living inside of every true child of God. Let me ask you, *"What do we need to do, as far as our relationship is concerned with Him?"* This is the most important question that we can ask. It's the same thing that the early Church had to do. Let me give you a couple of things:

Listen To Him

In order to listen, we must first be quiet. There is so much noise going on around us that it is really hard for us to quiet down and concentrate on listening to the Holy Spirit, but it is something that we must get into a habit of doing. Developing a habit throughout the day of really quieting down, tuning into the Holy Spirit and listening to what He wants to say to us. This is what the early Church had to do.

"Pastor Matt, how does He speak to us?" Let me help you.

1. The Word

What we have today, that the early Church did not have, is the Word of God, and the more you fill your mind and saturate your life with the Word of God, the more Jesus can speak to you. He can speak to you as you read it, and He can recall it to memory after it's been lodged in your heart.

2. The People of God

He also speaks through the people of God. This has happened many times in my life when someone says something to me and I know it is directly from the Lord. Has this ever happened to you? God often uses His people to speak, just as He used others throughout the New Testament to encourage, rebuke, correct and discipline.

3. The Voice of God

This is another way that He speaks to us. He gently whispers to those who are listening. Does He really? Think about this: Do we have Jesus speaking in the Word of God while He was on this earth? Yes. He says, *"My sheep hear my voice,"* and we have to listen to Him, but we have to get to a place where we can hear Him. Do you understand that? It's so important in the life of every Christ-follower. Turn off the radio. Turn off the noise. Turn off the smart phone. Carve out time to be quiet before the Lord. He wants to speak to you, and what He says will never contradict what has been said in the Word of God.

Obey Him

You must listen to Him, and you must obey Him. I told you earlier that the Holy Spirit, the Spirit of Jesus, can be grieved. Do you know you can make Him sad and angry? Do you know that His power can be cut off? The Apostle Paul on multiple occasions clearly says for us not to do that.

"And do not grieve the Holy Spirit of God, with whom you were sealed for the day of redemption" (Ephesians 4:30, NIV).

To grieve means to make sad or sorrowful. This verse is actually is a picture of Jesus recessing to be alone and be sad. If you read in the Gospels, do you ever see Jesus grieved? Do you see Him weeping? Yes.

Why? Sinful choices, hardened hearts, and most often disbelief. Paul in this passage, writing to the Ephesian believers, says don't do anything that will make the Holy Spirit sad.

"Do not quench the Spirit" (1 Thessalonians 15:19, NIV).

To quench means to cut off or suppress, and our disobedience to Jesus actually cuts off His power that is operational in our lives. What then does a Christian's life look like as he lives with a grieved or quenched Holy Spirit living on the inside? It looks exactly the same as a person who does not know God at all! At that point, he ceases walking in the life and power of Jesus and he walks according to his own power, just like an unbeliever!

This is why the Holy Spirit cannot be grieved or quenched by our unrepentant sin, disobedience or unyielding attitude. Jesus has to be seen and known in our lives.

Be Filled With Him

This is what the Apostle Paul tells the Ephesian believers:

"Don't be drunk with wine, because that will ruin your life. Instead, be filled with the Holy Spirit" (Ephesians 5:18, NLT).

Why does Paul parallel being filled with the Spirit with not being drunk with wine? Why doesn't he say, *"Don't steal or don't lie, but be filled with the Spirit?"*

Do you know what alcohol does to your body? Too much alcohol makes you speak differently, think differently, process differently, and walk differently. It influences your every movement and thought. This is the way it should be for every true believer when controlled by the influence of the Holy Spirit. The Holy Spirit should make us speak differently, think differently, desire differently, walk differently and live differently.

Being filled with Jesus includes every area. Paul is talking about making Jesus Lord. He's talking about being filled up completely with Jesus so that only He is seen and that only He remains. Do you understand that this is a relationship with Jesus living in you, where you lay down on the altar of surrender every day and every moment? It is saying to Him on a daily basis,

"Okay, Jesus. Here I am. Burn away everything in me that doesn't look like You. Take over my body, my mind, my will, my emotions. Live Your life through me."

Depend On Him

He is the God of the universe! Depend upon Him for all your needs.

Manley Beasley, an old, country preacher from Texas, lived in a broken body. At the end of his life, his body became so deteriorated with disease that he couldn't walk any more. When he preached, they had to carry him and his wheelchair on the platform.

He would often say something like this during his sermons. *"For what are you depending on God in your life in such a way that if He doesn't come through, you're sunk?"* He would go on to say that this kind of utter dependence upon God is how we should operate at all times in the Christian life.

In the book, *The Hiding Place*, Corrie Ten Boom writes about the horrors that she and her sister, Betsie, endured during World War II as they were placed in a Nazi Concentration Camp. On one occasion, feeling all alone and calling out for human help, Corrie comes to the realization that Jesus is all she needs. She admits to the Lord her foolishness for calling out for human help when so clearly, He was with her in that dark place. It was in this moment that Corrie finally came to realize that Jesus was her true hiding place. [2]

He is the resource that we need. We don't really need all the other stuff, just like the early Church understood. Get quiet before Him, listen to

Him, obey Him, be filled with Him, and depend upon Him for your every need.

Right now, ask Jesus to fill you. Ask Him to live mightily in you and control every part of you. Surrender to Him as Lord and Master. Ask Him to bear His fruit in you and live His life in you. This is what the Church needs moving forward, and what the culture desperately needs to see. It needs the people of God, not just the Pastors, listening to Jesus, obeying His every word, and depending mightily upon Him.

Faced with uncertainty about in which direction the Church needs to travel, let's go back all the way to where it all began: the reliance on the Holy Spirit. He is really the only Source that we have ever needed.

[1] Alan Hirsch, *"The Forgotten Ways: Reactivating The Missional Church."* (Brazos Press, Grand Rapids, Michigan 2006), 18.

[2] Corrie Ten Boom with Elizabeth and John Sherrill, *"The Hiding Place: 35th Anniversary Ed."* (Chosen Books, Grand Rapids, Michigan 2006), 170.

Chapter 13

MARKS OF THE EARLY CHURCH

"Church" is not going to a building and watching something. Neither is church staying at home and watching something on TV or on the internet. Since when did church ever become about watching something? If that's all it is, we've missed it! The Church is all about community. It's all about community.

Recently, I was talking with a friend of mine that used to attend the local church body that I pastored. He left when I was fired as did many people. He told me about the place where he and his family are now attending. *"We love the music and the speaker is really good too."*

I gently asked him, *"Are you involved in community?"*

"No."

I then said to him, *"If community is not involved, then it's not church. It's entertainment."*

He understood.

For millions of people in the United States, this is what church has become, watching something. They drive to a church, absorb and leave and they say, *"Well, I did my thing,"* or they sit at home and watch something and they say, *"Well, I did my thing,"* and nothing could be further away from the model of the New Testament because the New Testament is all about community.

Do you know right now, I believe more than ever, that people are craving community? Think about this: we live in a world where communication primarily takes place through the means of instant messaging. We live in a fast-paced world where we are rushing around from place to place or from event to event often to the point of exhaustion making it difficult for relationships to even exist. We live in a world where we are characterized by WHAT we do and how well we do it rather than being characterized by WHO we are and HOW we are doing. We live in a world where we've been conditioned to keep things on a surface level of politeness, *"Hi, how are you?" "Good to see you,"* but to keep people at bay from knowing who we really are or what we've done or what we are currently doing.

I want to take us back, all the way to the beginning of the Church to see how the people of the early Church embraced and ran after community, rather than running from it. If you remember, in the very beginning, the Holy Spirit came on the day of Pentecost. The disciples were indwelled by the Holy Spirit, the mark of true conversion, and were turned from being scared men, hiding behind closed doors, to being men of boldness. They began to witness to the community the reality and the power of the Resurrected Christ.

At this time in the life of the Church, you have this short window where there is no persecution. Acts 2 and Acts 4 capture what it was like in the beginning, and I believe these marks of Biblical community are to characterize the Church for the rest of its days, until Jesus comes back to make it whole and purify it completely.

Let's look first in Acts 2:

"Then Peter continued preaching for a long time, strongly urging all his listeners, "Save yourselves from this crooked generation!" [41] *Those who believed what Peter said were baptized and added to the church that day—about 3,000 in all"* (Acts 2:40-41, NLT).

Peter preaches publicly and powerfully on the day of Pentecost, and thousands believe and are baptized. Let me remind you who is in Peter's audience as he preaches. Jews are listening to his message because he addresses them and charges them with being complicit in the crucifixion of Jesus. He tells them, at one point in his sermon,

"But God knew what would happen, and his prearranged plan was carried out when Jesus was betrayed. With the help of lawless Gentiles, you nailed him to a cross and killed him" (Acts 2:23, NLT).

What boldness! Not only do you have Jews there, but you also have people there from all over the Aegean Sea region, the province of Asia, North Africa, the Middle East, and Rome as stated in verses 7-11 of chapter 2. The text says that many people, from all over the region, believed and were baptized as a result of Peter's preaching.

Notice what happens next:

"All the believers devoted themselves to the apostles' teaching, and to fellowship, and to sharing in meals (including the Lord's Supper), and to prayer. [43] *A deep sense of awe came over them all, and the apostles performed many miraculous signs and wonders.* [44] *And all the believers met together in one place and shared everything they had.* [45] *They sold their property and possessions and shared the money with those in need.* [46] *They worshiped together at the Temple each day, met in homes for the Lord's Supper, and shared their meals with great joy and generosity—* [47] *all the while praising God and enjoying the goodwill of all the people. And each day the Lord added to their fellowship those who were being saved"* (Acts 2:42-47, NLT).

The day of Pentecost, when the Holy Spirit indwelled the disciples, signifies the birth of the Church. Notice that right away, they immediately come together. What marked them? What marked the early Church as they began to live together right after Pentecost and the indwelling of the Holy Spirit within the hearts of men? 3 things:

Sound Teaching

"All the believers devoted themselves to the apostles' teaching" (Acts 2:42a, NLT).

Sound teaching from the Word of God is essential for spiritual growth. They devoted themselves to understanding God's Word. As stated before, you can't grow apart from the Word of God. Hopefully, we as believers know this by now.

Love For One Another

"Love for one another" is an overarching way to describe how this community operated, and it was characterized in two specific ways:

1. Fellowship

The text says that they worshipped at the Temple every day, they shared meals together in homes, and they enjoyed the company of one another. They loved being together. They loved being around each other. They enjoyed the company of each other, and that should definitely be a characteristic of God's people.

Jude 1:12 talks about these times of fellowship that involved food, calling them *"Love Feasts"* and that's what these meals were. They were received with love and enjoyment as they fellowshipped together.

Look at how the Apostle John talks about how we should love one another.

"Dear friends, let us continue to love one another, for love comes from

God. Anyone who loves is a child of God and knows God. [8] But anyone who does not love does not know God, for God is love. [9] God showed how much he loved us by sending his one and only Son into the world so that we might have eternal life through him. [10] This is real love—not that we loved God, but that he loved us and sent his Son as a sacrifice to take away our sins. [11] Dear friends, since God loved us that much, we surely ought to love each other. [12] No one has ever seen God. But if we love each other, God lives in us, and his love is brought to full expression in us" (1 John 4:7-12, NLT).

"We surely ought to love each other." Why should love for one another characterize the New Testament Church? Who is the common denominator in that equation? The Holy Spirit. The Holy Spirit in me is drawn to the Holy Spirit living in you and there is an immediate connection and bond like you've known someone for years. John writes that when we love one another, truly love one another, God's love is brought to full expression in us.

2. Generosity

"And all the believers met together in one place and shared everything they had. [45] They sold their property and possessions and shared the money with those in need" (Acts 2:44-45, NLT).

They loved one another through fellowship, and they loved one another through generosity. They shared everything that they had (food, possessions, property, money) with those in need. Acts 4 elaborates on this in more detail.

"All the believers were united in heart and mind. And they felt that what they owned was not their own, so they shared everything they had. [33] The apostles testified powerfully to the resurrection of the Lord Jesus, and God's great blessing was upon them all. [34] There were no needy people among them, because those who owned land or houses would sell them [35] and bring the money to the apostles to give to those in need" (Acts 4:32-35, NLT).

Did you notice the mindset of the early believers? *"They felt that what they owned was not their own"* and *"there were no needy people among them."*

That goes against everything we've been taught living in a Western, prosperous, mindset, doesn't it? It sounds a lot like socialism, except that it is not government forced but voluntarily given from a generous, loving heart.

"Pastor Matt, can't people take advantage of that system?"

Yes. That's why it says in other parts of the New Testament that if a man refuses to work, he was not to receive any food. It also says to put people like that out of the Church so that they can learn to be productive.

But, right here we have a picture of Biblical community characterized by true generosity. This should be one of the core values of the people of God: generosity and giving.

Imagine if we reversed the arrows when it comes to giving, and we sent people out and gave them their tithes to manage. What if we trained them to meet the needs of the neighborhood, the community, the city, the county, the state, the nation and the world? What if the tithe did not go to building programs and capital campaigns and bricks and mortar and maintenance? What if instead it went towards missions and ministry?

Think about all of those resources leveraged in the Kingdom of God for Kingdom work! Think about all the resources being freed up to actually change the world because God's resources are being used God's way!

Imagine if someone in your micro church body lost their job. You could use those resources to take care of that family. If someone had an illness and medical bills, your church body could provide for them. If someone in the community was in need of assistance, your church body could tangibly show them the love of Jesus. If there was a need in the world, your church body could meet it

This is the way that it is designed to be according to the New Testament. Read again Acts 2 and Acts 4. Generosity was to be shown to those in need.

When you give to a traditional model church, to where does all of that money go? It goes to building funds, building maintenance, insurance, electricity, A/C, staff salaries and on and on. I've heard David Platt, the former director of the International Mission Board, say that the average church in North America gives .05% to global causes. Not 5% but .05%. That shocked me when I heard him say that. Is this what God has in mind for His resources?

I previously wrote that less than 9% of born-again believers tithe. Think about this, *"Should you give more, now that you are under grace, as opposed to being under the giving demands found in the law, or should you give less?"*

Writer Mike Holmes addresses what would happen if Christians were to start giving a minimum of 10%. According to Holmes, the $165 billion that would become available could be used this way:

$25 billion could relieve global hunger and eliminate deaths from preventable diseases within five years.

$15 billion could solve the world's water and sanitation issues—specifically in places where a majority of people live on less than $1 a day.

$12 billion could end illiteracy.

$1 billion could fully fund all overseas mission work.

$100–$110 billion would be left over for additional ministry needs. [1]

Instead of resources being utilized on buildings and building maintenance, what if there was something different? What if the majority of the money actually was given back to the people for THEM to distribute? The Church could actually live out Acts 2 and 4, and the world could be blessed.

During the 2020 pandemic, I served on the *Children's Hope Chest* Board of Directors. The vision of Hope Chest is unique, unlike anything I've ever seen. They connect an organization in the West (local church body, business) with an impoverished community overseas. It is a partner to partner relationship that focuses on whole transformation of the community and eventually graduation! They literally have an end date in mind for the community to be self-sustaining! They operate in some of the most destitute places on the planet, focusing on Isaiah 1 and James 1 as they take action to care for the orphan and widow.

Do you know what happened starting in 2020? Their resources dried up. Churches started holding back and telling them, *"No,"* and cutting the orphan and widow out of their budget because, *"We have to take care of the needs of Americans in our communities."* Let me ask you:

"Compared to global poverty, how impoverished are Americans?"

Every American is rich, multiple times over compared to people living in the undeveloped parts of the world, and if you don't believe me, go. Go where I have been. Go to the slums of Guatemala City where 15,000 live in the city dump and scavenge through the trash. Go to Haiti. Go to the slums of Africa and see it for yourself. I honestly wish every American could do it.

One church body in our area during the pandemic decided to spend $250,000 of their budget for the express purpose of giving every teacher in our area a $50 gift card to *Target*. Was it a nice gesture? Sure. Compared to the impoverished world, did the people in our suburbia area *"need"* a $50 gift card? Not on your life!

Another church body in our area spent $3,000,000 to expand their parking lot. Really? Really? Do you know what three million dollars could do around the globe?

The giving shortage that Hope Chest had to endure during the pandemic caused them to, get this, shift all of their focus away from partnering with churches to partnering with businesses! Businesses were now being looked upon to take care of the widows and orphans around the world! Do you think God is happy about that? For a fact, He is not. He is angry. We have wasted the resources that He has entrusted to our care.

Prayer

The early Church devoted themselves to prayer. When someone was sick, they prayed. When someone was in trouble, they prayed. When someone was being sent out, they prayed over them. When someone had a need, they prayed. When they encountered spiritual warfare, they prayed. They prayed as if their life depended upon it, that if God didn't come through for them, they were sunk. They saw God as the only One who could truly take care of them.

Again, this is why God caused the Church to remain on a micro-level. It was so that they could know the needs of one another and fervently pray for each other.

Let me give you two verses found in Isaiah 62.

"O Jerusalem, I have posted watchmen on your walls; they will pray day and night, continually. Take no rest, all you who pray to the Lord.
7 Give the Lord no rest until he completes his work, until he makes Jerusalem the pride of the earth" (Isaiah 62:6-7, NLT).

"Take no rest" and *"give the Lord no rest"* until He answers. Do we view prayer in this way? I think we often set about DOING what can be done in our own power and effort, and then we pray as a last resort. But the early Church DEVOTED THEMSELVES TO PRAYER. *"We will not rest and we will not let You rest, O Lord, until You answer our prayer."* Wow! What faith!

Are there some things in your life about which you are unwilling to let the Lord rest? Are there some things that you are unwilling to let go of until God answers? Then pray this way, like the early Church.

The Difference

What was the result of living in community? What happened among them as they devoted themselves to Sound Teaching, Genuine Love For One Another and Prayer? What made the difference? Two things:

Awe

"A deep sense of awe came over them all, and the apostles performed many miraculous signs and wonders" (Acts 2:43, NLT).

The presence of God came near as they lived in community with one another. Do you know that the more you draw near to God, the holier He becomes? Do you know that the closer you are to Him, the more you reflect Him? Do you know that the more you are around Him, you begin to act like Him? God moved mightily among them and through the apostles as they ministered to one another in community, and because He was so tangibly close, they lived in the AWE and blessings of God. God poured Himself out on them because, I believe, they valued community just like He does.

Addition

"...all the while praising God and enjoying the goodwill of all the people. And each day the Lord added to their fellowship those who were being saved" (Acts 2:47, NLT).

They devoted themselves to the Word of God. They devoted themselves to loving one another through fellowship, generosity and praying together, and God grew the church. God increased it. It was not by might nor by power but by the Spirit of the Living God working in them and among them.

Do you know why we don't see much awe and addition in our churches today? Do you know why we don't really see the transformation of communities and neighborhoods around us and throughout the impoverished world? It is because we've neglected the foundational marks found in Acts 2 and 4 to which the early Church devoted themselves. They embraced real, genuine community with one another that motivated them towards love and good deeds.

This is why we must reverse the arrows and show this love to a lost and dying world, creating community where there is none. Then, everyone can rejoice in the awe of God and the addition of people into the Kingdom of God.

[1] Mike Holmes, *"What Would Happen If the Church Tithed?"* (Relevant Magazine, June 15, 2021). www.relevantmagazine.com.

Chapter 14

BIBLICAL COMMUNITY

Before the Covid-19 shutdown, my family attended a church body in our area. We occasionally do that from time to time so that we can get to know the people in our community. During our visit to this church body, my wife and I attended a Sunday School class where all the chairs were set up in rows. This allowed us to only see the back of each other's heads. I thought this was kind of a strange way to develop community, but we sat down nonetheless. Next, we all listened to a video sermon, just as if we were listening to a Sunday morning preacher. After that, we discussed the sermon a little bit, prayed and then were dismissed.

In this context where we were hoping to meet and get to know people, we didn't really get to meet anyone. When it was all over, most of the people went into the larger auditorium, sat in rows all facing forward, and listened to another sermon.

We literally went from a *"small church experience"* to a *"large church experience"* that was all focused on the same thing: Information! Was it informative? Yes. Was it an educational experience? Yes. Did we experience Biblical community? No, and I'm afraid this is the norm for many, many churches.

In America, we want information. We want entertainment, but Biblical community? That's getting a little too close for our comfort. I want to expound on this idea of community and show you just how interwoven this early community of believers was as found in the New Testament. Community literally permeated every part of their lives. Every part.

Meat Sacrificed To Idols

Look first at the Corinthian believers as they dealt with the reality of eating meat sacrificed to an idol. *"Pastor Matt, what does eating meat sacrificed to an idol have to do with community?"* Let me explain.

Emperor worship and idol worship enveloped the Roman Empire. A Roman official serving under Emperor Nero in the first century, once said of Athens: *"Truly our neighborhood is so well stocked with deities to hand, you will easier meet with a god not a man."* [1] This is why Paul, as he walked through Athens, was shocked to read an inscription to *"an unknown god."*

He made this *"unknown god"* the centerpiece of his eloquent speech given on Mars Hill. As I stood on Mars Hill, I imagined what it was like for him as he explained to the learned the One for whom they ultimately longed, the Maker of Heaven and earth.

The early Church was birthed into this environment of Emperor worship and idolatry. Imagine living during that time as a believer and being invited over for dinner at the home of someone who's not. You know that they will have an idol somewhere in that house because every house that was not following The Way had one.

Suppose, before they serve anyone food, they first scoop out a little bit of the meal and dedicate it to the idol in their house by putting some food at its feet. Then, they serve everyone else food. What's running through your mind as a believer? *"Does this now mean that this meal is dedicated to a false idol?" "Is this meal spiritually contaminated?" "Am I being displeasing to God by partaking in this meal that has been dedicated to and idol?"* Genuine questions.

Let me give you another example. Suppose you had a best childhood friend who left when he was eighteen years old to serve in the Roman military. During the time that he is away, you choose to follow Christ. Let's say he returns, not knowing you are a believer. Upon seeing you, he opens his wine bottle and pours a little out on the ground as a libation, a drink offering to the gods. He then takes a swig and then offers the bottle to you. What do you do? Do you drink knowing that what you are drinking has first been offered in honor to the false, pagan gods? Do you tell him that you can no longer do that because you are now a follower of Christ, at the risk of imprisonment or even death? These were real life, every day scenarios for believers living in the pagan Roman Empire.

Let me give you a third example. When the Church came on the scene, right after Pentecost, you had Jews who believed the message about Christ and you had Gentiles who believed. And now, they were coming together to form one new body, a new society of people marked by faith in Jesus and the indwelling Holy Spirit.

In the market place, it was common for meat to be sold that had first been dedicated as a sacrifice to a false god prior to its sale. The Jews would have nothing to do with such meat, believing that to partake of falsely consecrated meat was to give approval of idol worship and actually eat the food of idols.

The Gentile believers often rejected the thinking of the Jews concerning this matter because they believed that they could eat meat that had first been sacrificed to idols without endorsing idolatry because they had not actually been the one who offered the sacrifice. This had become such an issue in the early Church that the Apostle Paul had to address it.

"Now regarding your question about food that has been offered to idols. Yes, we know that "we all have knowledge" about this issue. But while knowledge makes us feel important, it is love that strengthens the church" (1 Corinthians 8:1, NLT).

What's he saying? He's saying in a very broad way, that it is all about the community of faith, not what you individually believe about this subject. He continues.

"But you must be careful so that your freedom does not cause others with a weaker conscience to stumble. [10] *For if others see you—with your "superior knowledge"—eating in the temple of an idol, won't they be encouraged to violate their conscience by eating food that has been offered to an idol?"* (1 Corinthians 8:9-10, NLT).

"Weaker conscience?" "Violate their conscience?" What's going on here? This is what Paul is saying, *"If they see you eating, won't they be encouraged to join you and do as you do, even though they believe it to be wrong?"* That choice would then *"violate their conscience."* Look at verses 11 and 12.

"So because of your superior knowledge, a weak believer for whom Christ died will be destroyed. [12] *And when you sin against other believers by encouraging them to do something they believe is wrong, you are sinning against Christ"* (1 Corinthians 9:11-12, NLT).

Who is the weaker brother in this context? It was the Jewish believer. Who has the *"superior knowledge?"* The Gentile believer. Paul uses tough language, here. Did you read it? Something is considered to be sinful to other believers because of your behavior. Your choices might encourage someone to copy your behavior even though they know it's wrong for them to do it. In other words, your spiritual health is connected to their spiritual health in every choice you make. Look closely to what the Apostle Paul says next in vs 13. Don't miss this.

"So if what I eat causes another believer to sin, I will never eat meat again as long as I live—for I don't want to cause another believer to stumble" (1 Corinthians 9:13, NLT).

Paul says that he will limit his freedom forever in order to preserve unity in the body of Christ.

Let me give you an example of what this should look like today in the life of the church body.

Drinking alcohol would be a great example of a gray matter. Is it specifically forbidden in Scripture? No. Could it cause someone to stumble? Yes.

I've told my children why my wife and I don't drink. One reason is the answer to this question: *"Is alcohol in the home and being consumed by us what we want we want to reap in our children?"* We've said, *"No. It's not worth it."*

All four of our children are still living at home, and that's not the example that we want to provide for them because we know that what we often display for them will be reaped in them.

Secondly, if I being a leader in the church were to have alcohol in a public place, could that cause someone to stumble? Could someone say, *"Well, if Pastor Matt drinks then I guess it's okay?"* Could I unknowingly cause someone to sin, by encouraging them to do as I am doing? Absolutely. But you say, *"Yes, but Pastor Matt, the Bible doesn't forbid it."* Read vs 13 again.

"So if what I eat causes another believer to sin, I will never eat meat again as long as I live—for I don't want to cause another believer to stumble" (1 Corinthians 9:13, NLT).

It's not about whether or not eating meat sacrificed to an idol or drinking alcohol is allowed or not allowed, it's all about living within the community of faith and making choices within the context of the community of faith. Paul says about this issue, *"I will never eat meat again as long as I live."*

"Pastor Matt, is every choice I make to be viewed within the context of the community of faith?" Now you are getting it. Yes!

Look at 1 Corinthians 10 as Paul continues in this matter.

You say, "I am allowed to do anything"—but not everything is good for you. You say, "I am allowed to do anything"—but not everything is beneficial. [24] *Don't be concerned for your own good but for the good of others* (1 Corinthians 10:23-24, NLT).

"Don't be concerned for your own good but for the good of others." That's what Paul says. This is huge! Our gray matters today need to be treated the same way as the issue of meat sacrificed to idols back then because it is all about living in community with one another.

When I went to Africa for the first time, I did so with a group of Pastors from all over the Southeast. There was one group of young guys, all from the same church, (one Lead Pastor and his two associates) that stood out to everyone because they made it a point to publicly and loudly flaunt their Christian *"freedom"* in front of all who were on our trip, including all of the people who were outside of our group which included our African brothers and sisters. How did they publicly and loudly flaunt their Christian freedom? By doing a lot of loud cussing and a lot of drinking, heavily. It was to the extent that it became uncomfortable for a lot of us to be around. I played college baseball, and I'm familiar with guys using bad language. The language that these *"Pastors"* used on this trip, was worse than any foul-mouthed pagan teammate that I have ever played with.

These Pastors' immature behavior, in essence, was saying, *"MY Christian freedom allows ME to do anything I want!"* Paul would say to them, *"Wrong! It's not about YOUR freedom but the community of faith and living in love toward one another. Don't be concerned for your own good but for the good of others."*

What the New Testament is teaching us through meat sacrificed to idols is that every decision we make, every decision, should be based on the community of faith. *"How will this decision affect those in the Body of Christ?"* This was the mindset of the early Church as they relied on the Holy Spirit.

The Lord's Supper

Think once again about the Lord's Supper found in 1 Corinthians 11. Read it. You will see what Paul was so upset about with the Corinthian believers. They turned the meal into a selfish endeavor, not a meal centered on community.

For the average mom, what is her most treasured time with her family? The time spent around the dinner table. She wants to see all of those little faces around her table, and she guards that time to the best of her ability. How long would she put up with people arriving late to the table, not sharing the meal equally? How would she feel about some of her children receiving food and some going hungry? How would she feel as her children argued and squabbled with each other the whole time? How would she feel about them getting up and leaving the table anytime they felt like it? This was the Corinthian Church.

What was the ultimate message Paul was telling the Corinthian believers concerning the Lord's Supper? The same thing any mother would say. *"It's not about you! It's not about eating food. It is about the community of faith as expressed in love for one another. It is about putting each other's needs above your own, waiting for one another and serving one another."* The message is clear. We arrive to the meal as individuals, but we gather as a family.

I could mention other examples, like 1 Corinthians 5 where Paul tells the Corinthian believers that they are not to judge unbelievers, those outside the community of faith, but that every believer should be judged to see if their faith is genuine. The point of the passage? *"Those who claim Christ as their Master are now subject to the scrutiny of the church body."*

This sounds so foreign to us because we have bought into the Western mentality of minding our own business, but that is not a Biblical mindset when it comes to always living in community. Sometimes we need to confront and say some things in love, and sometimes we need to humbly receive it.

Let me give you one last example of real community that might be a little uncomfortable to take in.

Confession

James, the brother of Jesus, tells us that in order for healing and freedom from sin to occur, there must be confession of that sin to those within the body.

"Confess your sins to each other and pray for each other so that you may be healed" (James 5:16, NLT).

I can hear it now. *"Confess my what, to whom?"* Let me ask you, does anyone know your sins and deepest struggles? Do you know anyone else's, so that you can pray for each other and be healed from those sins? This is what Biblical community looks like.

But we in our Western mindset still push back hard against the practice of confession. It sounds so foreign to our ears because we live in a society where the individual is celebrated, yet the Scripture is clear. Confession to others is the only way healing takes place in our lives.

Because the individual mindset is uplifted, the Christian mindset becomes, *"As long as I'm doing the right thing, as long as I am taking my family to church, as long as I'm growing in my faith, as long as my church is growing, as long as I'm going to Heaven, as long as I'm right with God, everything is okay."*

But, do you see in all of these Biblical examples that I've given you how intertwined these lives were commanded to be? Meat sacrificed to idols was a huge issue in the early Church. The Love Feast was a central part, every time they worshipped together. They were to be so acquainted with each other that they knew each other's struggles and sins. This is why Paul told them from the very beginning to *"bear each other's burdens."*

They were to journey along and help each other and call each other out and uplift each other and be known by others and truly know each other. They were to confess their sins to each other and pray for each other so that healing and maturity could take place.

Does this type of community exist in our churches and in your life as a follower of Jesus? The reason that we probably do not see it is because we've actually modeled our churches away from real community. The worship service is celebrated. The big gathering is upheld as the standard because that's where attendance numbers can really be tracked.

Even if you have *"small groups"* as a part of your church, how many really get down to the Biblical point of real community? This is why we have to reevaluate everything that we are doing in the traditional church model, because if it doesn't revolve around genuine Biblical community, it can't really be called a Biblical Church.

How do we get connected to people like that? How do we make their life my business and my business their life?

Intentionality

Community doesn't just happen. It has to be intentionally sought out. Who do you need to let in? Who do you need to seek out? Who do you need to share with? Who do you need to confess to? Who do you need to press into?

Consistency

Don't drift from it. The devil wants you to hide and pull back and withdraw and the devil wants you to sit back and mind your own business. Don't do that. Be constantly diving back into community.

You say, *"Pastor Matt, I'm too busy for relationships like that."* Read very carefully. Clear your schedule! The Christian life is to be lived out in the context of intertwined, all up in your business community, to the point that when you hurt, I hurt. When you rejoice, I rejoice. When you are in need, I help you. When you fall, I encourage you to get back up. When you are tempted, I pray for you. When you are out of line, I tell you and on and on.

Honesty

How often do we really let relationships get to that level, beyond the surface level to the matters of the heart? We need to foster this kind of living because we know that confession and transparency can lead to deeper levels of intimacy that can begin to set people free. Understand clearly. This is not about your own spiritual journey. It is all about the community of faith.

The best way to disciple people is not through the pulpit, as much as it pains me to write that. The best way is through community. Do you want your people to live righteously? Put them in community, and Pastor, with all due respect, it starts with you.

Celebrate the small in your church. Get back to the New Testament way of church, and revolve everything around that model, not the big worship service. When you do that, you will watch your people mature right before your eyes, and the pagan culture around you begin to change.

[1] Titus Kennedy, *"Athens."* Drive Through History Adventures, (September 12, 2018). www.drivethroughhistoryadventures.com.

Chapter 15

AN INVITATION TO THE TABLE

Living in the Southern part of the United States is a very unique experience. I was born in Pascagoula, Mississippi and I grew up in Mobile, Alabama, places that you would call the deep South.

The South is different, especially when it comes to *"Southern hospitality."* It's not just a phrase, it is a way of life. People are genuinely hospitable. We open doors for each other, say *"hello"* to perfect strangers, carry on lengthy conversations with people standing in the check-out line and start up another one with the cashier when it's our turn to pay.

It is customary to look people in the eye and acknowledging people with a wave or a nod or a spoken word. Social etiquette in the South is expected and that's just the way it is, or at least it used to be. A person who keeps to himself is considered rude where I come from.

Let me tell you why I bring that up. Southern Hospitality should be a characteristic of every person that names the name of Christ. As people come to Christ, God instills within them a genuine love for people, and that love is Biblically shown through the means of hospitality.

Hospitality literally means, *"The love of strangers."* The dictionary defines it as *"The friendly treatment of guests or strangers; an act or show of welcome."*

Do you know that God commands hospitality for the people of God? Let me show you first in the Old Testament.

"Do not take advantage of foreigners who live among you in your land. [34] Treat them like native-born Israelites, and love them as you love yourself. Remember that you were once foreigners living in the land of Egypt. I am the Lord your God" (Leviticus 19:33-34, NLT).

Concerning foreigners in the land of Egypt, hospitality was expected among the people of God because God had taken His people in and brought them into the land flowing with milk and honey. God had been hospitable to them, and they were now commanded to do the same for the foreigners living among them.

Think about the story of Ruth and Boaz. Boaz was wealthy. Ruth was poor. Ruth would go into his fields and work the corners of the fields and take home whatever she could harvest because the corners were commanded in Scripture to be left for the poor. This was the social welfare system that God set up in that day to take care of the needs of the impoverished.

In the Old Testament, travelers would also arrive in the town square at the end of the day and expect someone to invite them into their home, and they would be pretty offended if it didn't happen. This custom was still practiced in New Testament and Jesus tells a story about it.

Then, teaching them more about prayer, he used this story: "Suppose you went to a friend's house at midnight, wanting to borrow three loaves of bread. You say to him, [6] 'A friend of mine has just arrived for a visit, and I have nothing for him to eat.' [7] And suppose he calls out from his bedroom, 'Don't bother me. The door is locked for the night, and my family and I are all in bed. I can't help you.' [8] But I tell you this—though he won't do it for friendship's sake, if you keep knocking long enough, he will get up and give you whatever you need because of your shameless persistence" (Luke 11:5-8, NLT).

It's midnight, and a friend has arrived and there was nothing to eat. The host goes over to his neighbor's house and asks him for bread in order to provide food the midnight guest. Jesus tells us that this neighbor refuses to help! Everyone listening to Jesus would have gasped at this point. Refusing to help your neighbor, especially when a midnight guest is involved, is shameful behavior and it is still this way in much of the Middle East.

Hospitality was widely practiced in the Old Testament and commanded by God. It is no less talked about in the New Testament and is still commanded by God. Hospitality (the entertainment of people in the home) was expected to be a characteristic of every New Testament Christ follower.

"Don't just pretend to love others. Really love them. Hate what is wrong. Hold tightly to what is good. [10] Love each other with genuine affection, and take delight in honoring each other. [11] Never be lazy, but work hard and serve the Lord enthusiastically. [12] Rejoice in our confident hope. Be patient in trouble, and keep on praying. [13] When God's people are in need, be ready to help them. Always be eager to practice hospitality" (Romans 12:9-13, NLT).

Command: Always be eager to practice hospitality, to entertain guests in your home.

"Keep on loving each other as brothers and sisters. [2] Don't forget to show hospitality to strangers, for some who have done this have entertained angels without realizing it! [3] Remember those in prison, as if you were there yourself. Remember also those being mistreated, as if you felt their pain in your own bodies" (Hebrews 13:1-3, NLT).

Command: Don't forget to show hospitality to strangers.

"The end of the world is coming soon. Therefore, be earnest and disciplined in your prayers.

[8] Most important of all, continue to show deep love for each other, for love covers a multitude of sins. [9] Cheerfully share your home with those who need a meal or a place to stay" (1 Peter 4:7-9, NLT).

Command: Cheerfully share your home with people.

Hospitality was so important that it was a requirement for someone holding the office of elder, being a leader in the church body.

This is a trustworthy saying: "If someone aspires to be a church leader, he desires an honorable position." [2] *So a church leader must be a man whose life is above reproach. He must be faithful to his wife. He must exercise self-control, live wisely, and have a good reputation. He must enjoy having guests in his home, and he must be able to teach"* (1 Timothy 3:1-2, NLT).

"A church leader is a manager of God's household, so he must live a blameless life. He must not be arrogant or quick-tempered; he must not be a heavy drinker, violent, or dishonest with money. [8] *Rather, he must enjoy having guests in his home, and he must love what is good. He must live wisely and be just. He must live a devout and disciplined life"* (Titus 1:7-8, NLT).

Are you picking up the theme here? Everyone from the top down was commanded to make entertaining guests in their home a priority, and it was to be done cheerfully and with enjoyment! Let me ask you. Does this sound like the Church in the West today? Do we cheerfully look for people to host and invite over? Do we cheerfully open our homes for someone to sleep in or take in a meal? Yet, repeatedly, throughout the Old Testament and New Testament, we see this practiced and we see it commanded for the people of God. If we don't see it happening in our churches, once again, can we really call our model Biblical?

Why do you think God places such an emphasis on the home and the invitation for people into that environment? Let me give you a few reasons. When you practice hospitality, you are:

Being Like God

God loves to welcome strangers! This goes all the way back to the Old Testament when He chose lowly Israel to be His instrument of grace and the object of His affection, and it all points to the Gospel that we know and love.

"But you are not like that, for you are a chosen people. You are royal priests, a holy nation, God's very own possession. As a result, you can show others the goodness of God, for he called you out of the darkness into his wonderful light. [10] *"Once you had no identity as a people; now you are God's people. Once you received no mercy; now you have received God's mercy."* [11] *Dear friends, I warn you as "temporary residents and foreigners" to keep away from worldly desires that wage war against your very souls"* (1 Peter 2:9-11, NLT).

We are temporary residents and foreigners to this world because God has taken us in, saved us, adopted us as part of His family, and has blessed us with every spiritual blessing in Christ Jesus. We are no longer strangers to Him. We are one of His own.

God has set His affection and devotion on us who do not deserve it, and He extends His rich kindness towards undeserving sinners, as the Apostle Paul would say, *"Of whom I am the chief."*

Hospitality then is tangibly extending the grace of God that has been shown and extended to us.

Preparing For Heaven

"Then I heard again what sounded like the shout of a vast crowd or the roar of mighty ocean waves or the crash of loud thunder: "Praise the Lord! For the Lord our God, the Almighty, reigns.
[7] *Let us be glad and rejoice, and let us give honor to him. For the time has come for the wedding feast of the Lamb, and his bride has prepared herself.* [8] *She has been given the finest of pure white linen to wear." For the fine linen represents the good deeds of God's holy people.* [9] *And the angel said to me, "Write this: Blessed are those who are invited to the wedding feast of the Lamb." And he added, "These are true words that come from God"* (Revelation 19:6-9, NLT).

The culmination of God's hospitality is in welcoming those that He knows into His heavenly home. He invites us to dine around His celestial table at the wedding feast of the Lamb! What an underserved privilege, having our feet under the table of the Lord!

Blessing People Here on This Earth

Jesus told His disciples to rely on the hospitality of others when he sent them out, and they did because hosting a stranger was considered to be an honor. They were treated like an honored guest.

Elijah had a room built for him in Shunem by a wealthy couple. They added on to their house just for Elijah to have a place to stay when he passed through town.

The Apostle Paul, in writing to Philemon concerning a fellow believer named Onesimus, asked Philemon to prepare a guest room for him. Paul hoped to visit his friend Philemon very soon.

When I travel I have people that I love, and that I know love me, open up their homes and welcome me in like a son...Ken and Pam Sparks in Colorado Springs, John and Gayle Rector in Venice, Florida, Campbell and Patty Gaunt in Englewood, Florida and many other wonderful people. I am truly blessed by their genuine hospitality and love for me, and that's one of the blessings that comes from hospitality.

Creating Community

The overarching theme of the New Testament is the understanding that the Father has graciously welcomed us into His family, adopting us as His very own children. He pursued us. He went after us. Shouldn't the Church look more like that as we live out that Kingdom mindset here on earth? Shouldn't we be creating community in our neighborhoods where there is none? Isn't this what the Father has done for us?

What are some practical things can we do to begin obeying the Biblical command to be hospitable? Let me give you a few things to think about.

Living With Open Homes

This has to become our mentality. We have to have an open home mentality, having people around our tables and in our extra bedrooms. This is what God has done for us as He welcomes us into His family and around His table.

"Oh, but Pastor Matt, you don't know what my home looks like on the inside." Read carefully. I've been welcomed in homes from around the world made of mud walls and dirt floors, and I've been welcomed in homes with metal walls and tarp roofs. People don't care what your home looks like. They care what your heart looks like.

Karen Burton Mains, the author of *Open Heart, Open Home* tells a story about her issue with opening her home.

One morning she decided to sit down and read a novel instead of doing the house work. Of all the days to do that, a person from her church body stopped by. The house was a mess—dishes in the sink, toys everywhere, last night's newspaper all over the floor.

As she went to the door, she could hear her father's voice, *"Hospitality comes before pride."* She swallowed her pride and let the person from church in. After they sat down, this person said to Karen, *"I used to think you were perfect, now I think we can be friends!"*

That encounter forced her to write down all of the reasons that she did not practice hospitality, and then she put a "P" right beside each one that is because of pride. [1] That is a great exercise to do because we must begin living with an open home mentality.

Looking For People To Invite In

It is actively looking for people to invite and welcome and get to know. It is actively looking for people to take in. It is actively looking for people to show the love of God. Isn't this what God has done for us? Didn't He seek us out? We should be doing the same with others, and we are commanded to do so.

When we recently moved to a new state and a new city, my niece wrote us a letter soon after we arrived. Do you know what that letter was all about? Hospitality! She wrote,

"In a season of getting to know the community around you and allowing strangers into your home and your lives, I hope this will serve as an encouragement to you. I've been reading in John this week and a certain phrase keeps sticking out to me... 'Come and see.' This is what Jesus invites others to do. I pray that you are encouraged as you as a family invite others to your table...to 'come and see'."

That was exactly what we needed to hear, and I believe the Lord was speaking directly to us through our niece. That letter stays near our dining room table where we can see it, as a constant reminder that we need to be looking for people to invite over and pursue.

How do you do that? You may have to schedule hospitality—like Sunday lunch or Friday dinner. Designate a day and look for people to invite over. The idea of hospitality in the New Testament is that of being constant or persistent in practice. In other words, it should be a lifestyle. One of the ways to jump start that lifestyle is to build it into your routine and schedule.

Loving People As Jesus Has Loved Us

Hospitality is not done for the sake of getting anything out of it but for the sake of showing kindness and grace to those with nothing expected in return. It is offering them the finest meal. It is offering them the most comfortable bed. It is offering them your full attention. It is offering them the best of everything you have. This is what Jesus has done for us!

I truly believe that if we practiced hospitality like the Bible instructs us to, we would see many, many people come to Christ. This is how the early Church grew so fast! This is how the Gospel was clearly lived and shared. The love that they claimed to know was seen and evidenced in how they welcomed others.

Obey the command of Scripture. Live with an open home. Look for people to invite over, and love them with the love of Jesus.

God has taken us from being lost and has brought into his household as adopted children. He continues to show us unending grace. Let us imitate our Lord in every way, even in ways that might make us really uncomfortable, as we'll see in the next chapter.

[1] Karen Burton Mains, *"Open Heart, Open Home,"* (Intervarsity Press, Westmont, Illinois 2002), as quoted in www.blog.karenmains.com.

Chapter 16

BIBLICAL HOSPTITALITY

I was recently reminded of a story that I heard about a Catholic young man arriving in Jerusalem late on a Friday afternoon. What happens in Jerusalem late on a Friday afternoon? Sabbath, and the observance of Sabbath shuts everything down. No work is to be done.

The bus that was taking this man to his destination stopped running, and so did all the cabs. He had just geared himself up for a very long walk to get to his place for the night, when a kind family noticed him and asked about his situation. They told him to come in and be their guest of honor for their son's Bar Mitzvah. This Catholic man went into a Jewish home as the guest of honor, had a wonderful time, and 24 hours later was on his way again.

I heard another story about a man traveling in Spain who arrived at a tiny village late one night. The whole place was dark, and he was uncertain what to do. But then, he saw a light in the distance. It turned out to be the light of a monastery. He knocked and was welcomed and fed and given a place to sleep. The next day, after he was on his way again, he discovered that the monks, assuming he was destitute, had slipped some money into his pocket while he was sleeping.

By these two modern stories, it is no wonder that the writer of Hebrews talks about those who practice hospitality have *"entertained angels"* without even knowing it. These two stories are not random stories of random acts of kindness. No. This kind of hospitality is imbedded in a whole way of community life for most of the world.

As I wrote in the last chapter, I truly believe that if we practiced hospitality like the Bible instructs us to, we would see many, many people come to Christ.

Biblical hospitality is so much more than just one meal. Don't get me wrong, it is that. God loves us opening our tables to anyone, but I want Jesus to speak to this and clarify some things for us, and I want us to be stretched spiritually as we hear what He says about what genuine hospitality is all about.

In Luke 14, Jesus is invited to a dinner, and notice what He says to the dinner guests,

Then he turned to his host. "When you put on a luncheon or a banquet," he said, "don't invite your friends, brothers, relatives, and rich neighbors. For they will invite you back, and that will be your only reward.
[13] *Instead, invite the poor, the crippled, the lame, and the blind.*
[14] *Then at the resurrection of the righteous, God will reward you for inviting those who could not repay you"* (Luke 14:12-14 (NLT).

Jesus is telling His listeners about the kingdom of God. God invites into relationship those who could never pay Him back, and Jesus says for us to do the same. Did you notice who Jesus placed at the top of His guest list?

"Poor, crippled, lame, and blind."

Jesus says, *"Don't invite your friends...relatives, and rich neighbors." "Go for the ones that cannot pay you back and who don't deserve it."*

Do you know the story of David and Mephibosheth? It's found in 2 Samuel 9.

One day David asked, "Is anyone in Saul's family still alive—anyone to whom I can show kindness for Jonathan's sake?" (2 Samuel 9:1, NLT).

David is the king, and what does a king normally do with all of the people in the previous king's household? He kills them for fear of retaliation. He should want to eliminate anyone who would try to take back the kingdom. But, in this conversation, what is David requesting? *"Who is there in Saul's family that is still alive that I can show kindness to, for Jonathan's sake?"* He's not asking in order to harm anyone. He's asking so that he can bless.

After asking around, his servants find out that one of Jonathan's sons was still alive but who was crippled in both feet. David sends for him at once. His name is Mephibosheth. What does David do when Mephibosheth arrives?

"Don't be afraid!" David said. "I intend to show kindness to you because of my promise to your father, Jonathan. I will give you all the property that once belonged to your grandfather Saul, and you will eat here with me at the king's table!" (2 Samuel 9:7, NLT).

I can just hear the other people in the Kingdom saying something like this under their breath, *"David, David, David. Couldn't you just bring him here for ONE meal? I mean eating with the king is a high privilege and honor. After all, David, he's crippled. He can't walk. He can't do anything for you, and he will be a tremendous burden to you as you care for him."*

But that was not the mentality of David. David, in this moment, is filled with grace as he gives Mephibosheth all the land that once belonged to Saul and makes him a CONSTANT guest of honor around his dinner table.

What did Mephibosheth do to deserve all of this? Absolutely nothing. It is a wonderful picture of the grace of God that He richly pours out on us as sinners who do not deserve anything good.

Here's the connection. Hospitality in Scripture is most often associated with strangers, poor people, the isolated and our enemies. When that kind of love happens, we truly model who God is and what His Church should look like.

Is it messy? Yes.

Is it costly? Yes.

Is it pulling you out of your comfort zone? Yes.

Is it an inconvenience and even sometimes a heavy burden? Yes.

But here's the deal. I'm beginning to judge my godliness based not on what I believe but on what my beliefs cause me to do. If I refrain from foul language and foul movies and sex before marriage, but don't love my neighbor as I love myself, how will the Lord look at me?

Am I for opening my home to a stranger who needs a bed?

Am I for visiting a nursing home and sitting with those whom nobody visits?

Am I for giving away my material possessions to meet the needs of the poor around me?

Am I willing to live on little and give away much so that others can be blessed rather than myself?

Am I for volunteering my time to sit and have lunch and read with a student who gets no attention or supervision at home?

Am I for visiting those in prison that the world has seemingly forgotten?

Am I for adopting a child that nobody wants and everybody has passed over?

Am I for opening my home to a foster child?

"Pastor Matt, I don't have time to do anything like that! I've got ball games to get to. I've got choir practice to attend."

I understand all of that, having four kids of my own, but Christianity in the world's eyes is defined by what our beliefs cause us to do. *"You say you love me, but do you show me love?"* Doesn't that make the words of Jesus come alive when He says,

"In the same way, let your light shine before others, so that they may see your good works and give glory to your Father who is in heaven" (Matthew 5:16, ESV).

Hospitality in the truest Biblical sense, is us acting most like God. Godliness is not defined by what we believe. We are godly when we model what God does.

What Does God Do?

HE LOVES PEOPLE. HE WELCOMES THEM IN. HE BANDAGES THEIR WOUNDS. HE GIVES OF HIMSELF, AND HE DOES THIS OVER AND OVER WITH EVERY ONE OF HIS CHILDREN.

He doesn't just do this for the *"good people"* because there is no such thing as good people. He does this for the vilest of people which is exactly what we all are.

"...but God shows his love for us in that while we were still sinners, Christ died for us" (Romans 5:8, ESV).

While we were in the midst of our most awful season of sin and rebellion against God, God reached out to us, pursued us, loved us and died for us, and adopted us into His family after belief and trust in Him. Forever He treats us and treasures us as His most honored guest.

Do I need to tell you the story of the Prodigal Son as the Father lovingly waits, night and day, for his wayward son to return? And when his son returns, he heaps all of the shame upon himself so that the shameful son receives no shame.

Do I need to tell you the story of the Good Samaritan who bandaged the wounds and paid the hospital bill of someone who would consider the Samaritan to be a low-life, an out-cast, a second-class citizen?

What does hospitality really look like? It looks like God. It is a lifestyle of the great commandment to Love God and Love People. It is us opening our hearts and resources for the welfare of others—being ready as food, drink, shelter, comfort, and welcome for people. It is us inviting people into our homes and serving them and meeting their needs—the poor, the lame, the outcast, the one that everyone has forgotten and on whom everyone looks down, even our enemies. God does it without expecting anything in return. We are commanded to do the same.

It's not just *"a meal"* but rather inviting someone in who is a constant guest at your table, just like Mephibosheth was to David. It is a heart that understands that all we own is the Lords. We are simply stewards.

There's a story that Shane Claiborne tells in one of his books. Let me close with it.

"A married couple who were unable to have children happened to meet a woman who had found herself six months pregnant and homeless, so they invited her into their home. It proved to be such a beautiful experience that they decided to continue living together to help raise the new baby girl while the mother pursued her dream of going back to school to become a nurse. They have been living together for over a decade now. They are a family, and the baby is now a teenager and the mom a nurse. A heart-wrenching twist to the story is that the wife of the married couple is now very ill with multiple sclerosis, but now the nurse living in her home is caring for her, just as she had cared for the nurse and her baby." [1]

What a beautiful picture of love in action. Who needs Christians the most in our cities?

Single moms and childcare?

Lonely single adults?

Addicts?

The poor?

Widows/Widowers?

Foster children and orphans?

Teenagers in the foster care system?

Those who are homeless?

Those who are sick and disabled?

Outcasts?

Our enemies?

Neighbors that you don't like very much?

People you don't know very well?

Those from the LGBTQ community?

Hospitality is the visible witness that the Kingdom of God has come. God invites us to His table to eat and be filled. We don't deserve it. We don't earn it. He just does it. Are you and I truly modeling that? When will we truly understand that the *"Church"* is not a building but a body of people, an army of God who are ready work for His glory? Again, this is not just the Pastor's job to do this. It is everyone who names the name of Christ.

Hospitality is a reflection of God's character that comes from a life that has been transformed. It is a heart that has been touched by an awareness that God loves people and that loving God means God loving people through us.

If Covid has taught us anything, it has taught us that we need to reverse the arrows and truly love those who need it most. The need is great, and God wants us, His body, to meet it. More specifically, God wants you to meet it!

Shane Claiborne, *"The Irresistible Revolution: Living As An Ordinary Radical, First Ed."* (Zondervan Grand Rapids, Michigan 2006), 183.

Chapter 17

THE END OF THE WORLD IS COMING SOON, THEREFORE...

If the world was coming to an end in one year, what would you do? Think about it: If you know for a fact, in one year, the world is coming to an end, what would that next year look like for you?

"Pastor Matt, I'd quit my job, cash out, and spend my last dime doing what I want to do."

Some of you might say, *"I'd tell as many people about Jesus as possible."*

Still others, *"I'd quit how I'm living. I'd get right with God, and live out these final days obeying the Master."*

The New Testament talks about the end of the world, but it's not presented in a hypothetical way as a question but rather it is presented as a hardcore fact.

Look at 1 Peter 4 and see what it says.

"The end of the world is coming soon. Therefore..." (1 Peter 4:7a, NLT).

The Apostle Peter tells his audience that the end of the world is coming soon. Why? Why would he say that? What was happening during that time to prompt that kind of statement?

The early Church, with the tremendous amount persecution that they were constantly enduring, lived with the mindset that Jesus was set to come at any moment. They lived with the expectation that it would happen in their lifetime.

Did they know when Jesus would come back, and did they miss it? No. Look at Acts chapter 1.

So when the apostles were with Jesus, they kept asking him, "Lord, has the time come for you to free Israel and restore our kingdom?" [7] *He replied, "The Father alone has the authority to set those dates and times, and they are not for you to know.* [8] *But you will receive power when the Holy Spirit comes upon you. And you will be my witnesses, telling people about me everywhere—in Jerusalem, throughout Judea, in Samaria, and to the ends of the earth."* [9] *After saying this, he was taken up into a cloud while they were watching, and they could no longer see him.* [10] *As they strained to see him rising into heaven, two white-robed men suddenly stood among them.* [11] *"Men of Galilee," they said, "why are you standing here staring into heaven? Jesus has been taken from you into heaven, but someday he will return from heaven in the same way you saw him go!"* (Acts 1:6-11, NLT).

Peter is standing here during this moment. He is an eye witness to this event. What did he hear during this encounter? The dates and times for God to restore all things is *"not for you to know. The Father has set those dates and times. Someday, Jesus will return just like the way you saw Him go."*

What prompted Peter to write to the believers, *"The end of the world is coming soon"* was the simple fact that they fervently believed that Jesus could come back at any moment. They lived with the expectation that it could happen very soon. We as believers in the Lord Jesus Christ, living on this earth, should live with the same mindset and have the same expectation.

In light of this expectation, Peter uses one word. Did you catch it? *"The end of the world is coming soon. Therefore." "Therefore."* In other words, he's about to tell them exactly what to do in light of the end of the world coming soon, and here's why I bring this up. Everything he tells them to do all revolves around reversing the arrows! He tells them to focus on Biblical community, everything I've been addressing in this book! Notice what he tells them to do:

The End of The World Is Coming Soon, Therefore Pray Earnestly

"The end of the world is coming soon. Therefore, be earnest and disciplined in your prayers" (1 Peter 4:7, NLT).

The end of the world is coming soon, therefore, pray. Is that what you were expecting him to say? If you think back to what the early community of believers dedicated themselves to when the first church movement started in the book of Acts, they dedicated themselves to the apostle's teaching, to fellowship, to sharing in meals and to...prayer.

They devoted themselves to prayer, and Peter was in that group. Don't forget that. Jesus taught Peter to pray when he walked with Him, Peter saw Jesus praying while He was on this earth, and now here, Peter sees God moving through this early group of believers as they prayed.

We so underestimate the effectiveness and importance of prayer. I recently was reading an account of the revival that took place in Jamaica in the year 1860. I love reading about revivals. Do you know how it began? It began with Christians coming together and praying at the *"peep of day"* for revival. God showed up in a mighty way in September of that year and when it was through, tens of thousands had come to Christ.

A congregational minister summarized the results saying, *"It closed the rum shop and the gambling houses, reconciled long separated husbands and wives, restored prodigal children...crowded every place of worship, quickened the zeal of ministers, purified the churches, and brought many sinners to repentance."* [1] It all began with prayer.

Peter doesn't tell us what to pray for in light of the world coming to an end, but I want to remind you again about who is writing this letter. PETER. Remember what happened to Him in the Olive Grove when he was with Jesus and was asked to watch and pray?

They went to the olive grove called Gethsemane, and Jesus said, "Sit here while I go and pray."

33 He took Peter, James, and John with him, and he became deeply
troubled and distressed. 34 He told them, "My soul is crushed with grief
to the point of death. Stay here and keep watch with me." 35 He went on
a little farther and fell to the ground. He prayed that, if it were possi-
ble, the awful hour awaiting him might pass him by. 36 "Abba, Father,"
he cried out, "everything is possible for you. Please take this cup of
suffering away from me. Yet I want your will to be done, not mine."
37 Then he returned and found the disciples asleep. He said to Peter,
"Simon, are you asleep? Couldn't you watch with me even one hour?
38 Keep watch and pray, so that you will not give in to temptation. For
the spirit is willing, but the body is weak." 39 Then Jesus left them again
and prayed the same prayer as before. 40 When he returned to them
again, he found them sleeping, for they couldn't keep their eyes open.
And they didn't know what to say. 41 When he returned to them the
third time, he said, "Go ahead and sleep. Have your rest. But no—the
time has come. The Son of Man is betrayed into the hands of sinners.
42 Up, let's be going. Look, my betrayer is here!" (Mark 14:32-42, NLT).

Jesus is about to face the cruelty of the cross. He pleads with His Father to find another way to save sinful humanity. He prays for three hours and asks His disciples to pray with Him. What do they do? They fall asleep.

What was the reason that Jesus said to Peter and the other disciples to stay awake and pray? It was so that they would not give into temptation. What was the temptation? To fall away, to give into the sway of the enemy.

Notice what Peter says in 1 Peter 5.

"Be sober-minded; be watchful. Your adversary the devil prowls around like a roaring lion, seeking someone to devour" (1 Peter 5:8, ESV).

Before Peter and the disciples fell asleep in the Garden of Gethsemane, Jesus said this to Peter, *"Before this night is over, Peter, you will deny me three times that you ever knew Me."* Do you know what Peter said? *"NEVER."* Then he slept. Then he denied the Lord, and then he wept.

This is why Peter says to us in this letter, *"Facing the last days, be alert, stay awake and pray. Don't be deceived, don't give up in the face of temptation. Pray."*

Notice next,

The End of The World Is Coming Soon, Therefore Love Deeply

"Most important of all, continue to show deep love for each other, for love covers a multitude of sins" (1 Peter 4:8, NLT).

The world is coming to an end, therefore really love one another. Again, this is not something you would expect to be on the list, but here it is. Just like prayer, it's all about Biblical community. *"Don't just say you love each other. Really love them. Even when they do wrong to you, keep loving them. Live in forgiveness. Live overlooking faults. Live in constant fellowship."*

Go back to the ministry of Jesus, of whom Peter was an integral part. Remember what Jesus told the disciples at the Last Supper? I'm sure Peter never forgot.

"Dear children, I will be with you only a little longer. And as I told the Jewish leaders, you will search for me, but you can't come where I am going. [34] *So now I am giving you a new commandment: Love each other. Just as I have loved you, you should love each other.* [35] *Your love for one another will prove to the world that you are my disciples."*

[36] *Simon Peter asked, "Lord, where are you going?"*

And Jesus replied, "You can't go with me now, but you will follow me later."

[37] *"But why can't I come now, Lord?" he asked. "I'm ready to die for you."*

[38] *Jesus answered, "Die for me? I tell you the truth, Peter—before the rooster crows tomorrow morning, you will deny three times that you even know me"* (John 13:33-38, NLT).

Peter skipped right over the new commandment thing, and went straight for the details. *"What? Where are you going?"* After his denial and repentance, Peter probably reflected on what Jesus was trying to say to the disciples. What did Jesus say to them in this moment? *"Love each other in such a way that it will prove to the world that you belong to Me."* Wow! By truly loving one another, the world will take notice. In other words, it's a steadfast, lasting, enduring to the end kind of love, just like God gives to us.

Does this sound like the body of Christ right now? Do you think we truly love one another? How about people from other churches and denominations? Do we truly love them?

A while back, I had coffee with a Pastor in our town who had been there for about ten years. I was asking him about the other Pastors in our area, and he told me that he didn't really know many of them. I asked if there was any kind of Pastor gathering in the city, and he didn't know of anything. He did know that if any gathering was taking place, it would only include Pastors from an affiliated or common denomination.

I said to him, *"They don't really intermingle?"*

"No. Not really."

How about people in the Church that have wounded us and said hurtful things about us. Do we truly love them? Have you ever thought about someone in the church, *"If so and so is going to be in Heaven, I'd rather not go?"* I have.

I heard this the other day, and I can't get it out of my mind. *"The world needs to know that if it cuts us, we will bleed love."*

Do we bleed love when we are cut, or do we bleed anger, revenge, unforgiveness and hatred? This is what Peter is saying. In the last days, act like a family and bleed love. Act like a family that sticks together and loves each other and forgives each other. This is what the world desperately needs to see in the last days.

The End of The World Is Coming Soon, Therefore Share Joyfully

"Cheerfully share your home with those who need a meal or a place to stay" (1 Peter 4:9, NLT).

The world is ending soon, therefore, share your home with joy. There it is again. Another command that we didn't expect to be on the list. As we've stated in the previous chapter, hospitality is what brings the Gospel to action, physically demonstrating the love of Jesus. This is what is going to change the culture. It is God's people walking into the messy situations of those living around them and inviting those situations into their homes, with joy.

Peter mentions one more thing:

The End of The World Is Coming Soon, Therefore Serve Enthusiastically

"God has given each of you a gift from his great variety of spiritual gifts. Use them well to serve one another. Do you have the gift of speaking? Then speak as though God himself were speaking through you. Do you have the gift of helping others? Do it with all the strength and energy that God supplies. Then everything you do will bring glory to God through Jesus Christ. All glory and power to him forever and ever! Amen" (1 Peter 4:10-11, NLT).

This is how important your spiritual gift is. It's so important that Peter says, *"In light of Jesus coming back really soon, get busy using your spiritual gift."* Once again, Jesus' words had to be echoing in his mind as he wrote this passage.

"In the same way, let your light shine before others, that they may see your good deeds and glorify your Father in heaven" (Matthew 5:16, NIV).

In the last days, the world needs to see the body of Christ, functioning as a healthy, whole body. They need to see us tending to the needs of others by using our spiritual gifts. They need to see us speaking the truth boldly, but in love. They need to see us weeping with those who weep. They need to see us crossing denominational lines, loving THE CHURCH, not just our own. They need to see an activated people, enthusiastically serving others, bringing glory to God. They need to see a called out people who truly love others with the love and power of Jesus.

Think with me for one second. When Peter said, *"The end of the world is coming soon. Therefore..."* are these the things that you had in mind?

Prayer,

Really loving each other,

Sharing with those in need,

Using your spiritual gift to serve one another.

Is this what you expected him to say? No. Of course not. These things don't sound relevant in our fast-paced culture that rewards diligent work and humanistic efforts, but why are these things important to Peter in light of the end of the world coming soon? Stop for just a minute and think about it.

Because again, it describes authentic, genuine, Biblical community as found in Acts 2 and Acts 4. It describes people serving as found in Ephesians 4. God has promised to bless with His presence and with His power those that live this way. This is what will change the world, the *"micro"* movement, not the *"macro"* movement. What will truly change culture is when we see culture as the fertile ground of a rich harvest.

We cannot stay cloistered in the *"safety"* of our sanctuaries. Pastor, the Church must be sent out, armed with love, creating community where there is none. This is what God is calling the Church back to. Not entertainment, not productions, but community so that the world can take notice. People will be drawn to Christ as He is magnified and glorified and exemplified in all of His people.

"The end of the world is coming soon, therefore...embrace Biblical community."

Let me give you my final closing thought.

About a year after I was fired, I was lamenting in my bedroom to the Lord. *"Lord, what about all of those people who were hurt and who will not return and who will walk away from You? What about all of those people?"*

In that moment, the Lord gave me a picture of the earth, and brought this to my mind, *"How big is your former church in comparison to the globe?"* I said, *"It's miniscule, like a grain of sand."* Here was the message that came to my mind. *"It's not that I don't care about those people. I'm doing something greater in the earth,"* and what He is doing is bringing the Church back to the New Testament.

Are we willing to follow? Are we willing to courageously reverse the arrows? I heard so many people and so many Pastors lamenting about the year 2020. *"Oh, I just wish things could go back to the way they were before Covid-19!"*

What if God is trying to sovereignly get our attention and bring us back to the blueprint of the Church the way it existed for the first 300 years? What if He's sovereignly opening our eyes to walk a new path, reversing the arrows and seeing a different road? Will we be so bold to follow Him wherever He wants to take His Church in the area of maturity and making disciples? I pray that we will obey, and I pray for you, Pastor, that you will have the courage to reverse the arrows.

[1] E. Michael and Sharon Rusten, *"One Year Book of Christian History,"* (Tyndale House Publishers, Carol Stream, Illinois 2003), 545.

HOW TO STRUCTURE A NEW TESTAMENT CHURCH

I want to give you some practical help as you think about the New Testament Church and how you could transition your church into a sending church and a church that chooses to reverse the arrows.

Many churches, when the pandemic hit, ramped up their video capabilities. Pastors would dress up in their suits and preach to empty auditoriums and then broadcast that online to the congregation.

What did many of their people do? They grabbed a cup of coffee sat back and watched. What everyone missed was taking it one step further. We were so close to expanding our reach and mobilizing our people, and we didn't even know it! It would have been so easy to mobilize the people of God to set up their homes as churches, using the technology that was already supplied to them. Yet, all we could think about was going back to what was familiar to us.

Vision

Let me remind you once again of the vision. Instead of all of these people in neighborhoods leaving their neighborhood, where all of the lost and hurting people are, driving to different churches around the city and then coming back to these neighborhoods, what if we reversed the arrows and we sent everything that is experienced in a typical local church to those people and sent the people out to those living around them, just like they did in the New Testament!

We could turn houses, coffee shops, schools, offices, huts into churches and resource them to be the local church right where they are! Not an inflow into a building but an outflow into the places where we live and work, to where the people who need it most are.

Imagine people being sent out, ministering in Jesus' name, tasked with mowing their neighbor's lawn, baking them cookies, getting to know them and inviting them over. Imagine your people seeing their houses as a real churches. What if there were several families from your church that lived in the same neighborhood? What if they intentionally began working together to reach the whole neighborhood?

Imagine all of your people gathering back together once a month, bringing with them all of the people that they influenced and loved on with the Gospel. How big of a building would you need at that point? Imagine monthly gatherings all over the area because you couldn't fit everyone in the same building? See what I mean? This is the possibility of thinking smaller in order to get bigger.

What if signs were given to people who chose to make their home (or other environment) into a church? How many churches you would end up with? Instead of having one campus, you could potentially have dozens of campuses and for some, thousands of church campuses all over the city and all over the region.

Imagine also local bodies of believers (other churches) using this model and actually working together in this way. Imagine a regional gathering of all of those participating in this same model of church. Where in your city could that event be held as everyone from the body of Christ came together?

Imagine once a year, every person who is connected with the Box Church model (the reverse the arrows network that I've started) gathering together in one place. What would that event look like and where would it be held?

Don't you understand by now that the way to increase numerical growth is by getting smaller, not bigger? The way to increase spiritual growth is by getting people into smaller settings, not larger ones.

Instead of building things and thinking along those lines, why don't we use the thousands upon thousands of things that are already built? The next time you drive down your street, don't see other houses that people live in. Instead, see those structures as potential church plants because that's what they are.

"Pastor Matt, can't you do both? Can't you gather your people all together on Sunday and also send them out?" Let me caution you on this line of thinking. People will always choose what is most comfortable and familiar to them. You have to make a shift in people's minds in order to break them free of that comfort and familiarity. We get so *"Sunday-centric"* that we forget what Sunday is all about—GOING! You have to break the body out of this Sunday-centric mentality and force them to see *"going"* as the main objective.

Technology

How can we as Pastors replicate ourselves to a larger group of people? Through the means of technology.

The Apostle Paul was a pioneer. He was called by God to take the Good News of Jesus to the Gentiles. How could he accomplish such a massive task? He used the technology of his day. What was the technology of his day? Letter writing.

He wrote letters from other cites or from jail and sent those letters (the Epistles) to the congregations that were started, first to one and then passed on to others. This gave him the ability to communicate with them without being present with them. He was able to be in several places all at once, just by using the written word. Think about if Paul had access to the internet! He would definitely use it.

We have not even begun to leverage technology in our churches today! Answer this question, *"How many people in the United States have a smart phone?"* Why then would we not leverage technology as best as we can?

What if you supplied your people with everything they would get during a Sunday morning service, not for their watching enjoyment but for the purpose of being resourced to reverse the arrows? If you go to www.box.church, you can see that a worship service is already loaded and ready to go. It has a 5-minute countdown, an introduction, worship songs, a sermon and discussion questions at the end. It literally takes what happens in a Sunday morning environment and pushes it to the smart devices so that people can have church right where they are. Leverage everything you can in the area of technology in order to resource your people to be on mission and reverse the arrows.

Resources on the App, on Your Phone

What if you resourced the people in your church on their smart phones with a library of information that would help them to live out the Gospel right where they are? Think about the body walking around with a spiritual library right on their smartphone? This is one way to fulfill the mandate of Ephesians 4.

If you look at the Resource page of Box Church, you will find articles that show you how to share your faith, how to disciple someone, how to pray, how to find your spiritual gift, how to read the Bible and much more including parenting and marriage resources. It's literally a box of goods that can equip you to live out the Christian life, and equip you to equip others.

Community

Reversing the arrows is turning your home, your office, your local coffee shop into a church gathering so that you can create community where there is none, just like they did in the New Testament! It is all about reaching people who have yet to be reached and loving them and ministering to them as Jesus did.

When these micro-churches meet, we encourage them to make gathering together for a meal part of their community experience each week. Everyone is encouraged to bring something to the table. Children as well as adults gather together, and fellowship is enjoyed by all. It is a picture of the earthly family, and it is a reflection of the Christian life.

Include children within the context of everything you do. Include them in all the *"adult"* conversations around the dinner table and in answering questions after the message. Let them be right beside their parents as they worship. Let them start joining in the discussions! One of the children in our box, age ten, asked after the message in front of everyone, *"What exactly is spiritual warfare?"* We were able to talk more about that and help her understand. This is all a part of the discipleship system, as they learn in the context of Biblical community.

Another one of the kids in our group, age 11, asked this question: *"How can I trust that the Bible and science can exist together?"* It was a great question as we explored the answer together in the context of his parents and in the context of community.

Giving

Imagine giving your people permission to give away the tithe. Imagine them seeing a need and being able to meet it. Imagine Acts 2 and Acts 4 being lived out in the context of community. Imagine no needy people among them because those needs were taken care of by the body. Imagine global causes being taken care of as the body of Christ as a whole leverages wealth for the Kingdom of God. This could all happen if the majority of the tithe was distributed to the people of God.

Making Disciples

Remember, the task of making disciples is not just the job of the Pastor or the other church leaders. This is the job of every person in the Kingdom. The people of God must be sent out on mission. They must be trained to make disciples and held accountable to do so. They must be released in Jesus' name to the ends of the earth. Imagine what it would look like in the world-wide body of Christ if everyone in the body made disciple making top priority. Not worship. Not gathering. Not fellowship. Making disciples.

Think small to get big. Don't miss this. It is in this *micro* context that the New Testament makes sense. Don't gather a crowd. Rather, disperse your crowd to go to their neighbors. Bring them back together once a month along with all of the people that they've influenced for the Gospel.

Use technology to expand your reach. Let God's people go and watch them grow before your eyes! Use the attraction of your people in the area of good works in the community to expand the Gospel reach rather than using the gimmicks, giveaways and the attractional means of trying to get people into your church buildings.

Strategy

I recently challenged a Pastor to do something. I said, *"Grab a city map that shows all the streets and neighborhoods in your city. Then, identify everyone in your congregation by where they live. See where all of your people are on a map."*

What would be the purpose of doing this? There may be thirty homes in the same neighborhood that attend the same church body, and yet they may not even know they all belong to the same fellowship! What if you mobilized them to a certain home in their neighborhood that was set up as a church? What if you gave them the task of reaching their neighborhood? That neighborhood home would be packed when they gathered together, and they would immediately have thoughts of expansion. The neighborhood would begin to change if this many families started living in community with one another and started being mission-minded in their neighborhood.

What if churches also became training grounds for equipping the body? What if there was training on how to share their faith? What if they were trained to disciple someone? What if they were trained with the express purpose of sending them out? This should be the strategy of every church moving forward if we want to see the culture changed.

Think This Way

What if persecution came against the Church in the U.S.? What would you do if it became illegal for you to gather publicly? Begin structuring your church with this mindset. Not only will this cause you to think Biblically, it will also prepare us for what I believe certainly lies ahead.

Expect Pushback

People don't like getting out of their comfort zones unless they are forced. You are going to hear people say, *"I like gathering with the whole body every weekend,"* or *"Why do we need to change?"* Just remember that it is all comfort zone communication. In reality, you will lose people when you make the shift back to New Testament Christianity. People will jump ship when you reverse the arrows. However, don't let that scare you. Jesus had people who left him. So did Paul. Expect it and focus on the people who are far from God that will be reached for the Gospel.

Get Out of the Way, Pastor!

Pastor, with all due respect, you are more than likely the greatest hinderance to spiritual growth in your church body. If you do all the work, as the congregation expects you to do, they will sit back and lazily watch while you work yourself to exhaustion. If you are the only one who teaches, they will listen to you for their spiritual nourishment, and more than likely not learn to feed themselves.

The Church must be raised up and sent out! Pastors, in Jesus' Name, let His people go! Begin training them. Begin focusing people on spiritual maturity, going, and making disciples. Begin looking for people to raise up. Begin looking for people to train and equip. Begin looking for potential leaders. Give so much of the ministry away that you virtually work yourself out of a job. This is the New Testament model!

"But, what if people don't come back? What if they go somewhere else?" Once again, people are going to leave. We are all sinful creatures driven by, especially in this culture, what makes us happy and what best suits our preferences. Remember, they are all God's people, not yours. If they leave, God can see fit to oversee them and discipline them.

No Fear

When I was in Africa for the first time, I got to witness one of the wonders of the world, the great migration of wildebeests across the Masai Mara River. What some people wait for days to see, I got to see it within 30 minutes of arriving while eating a sack lunch in the Jeep! What did it take for the wildebeests to all jump in? One courageous animal. Once one jumped in, they all followed behind.

Do you know where I'm going with this? Be the one, courageous, Pastor! Be the leader. Dare to reverse the arrows in the church that God has allowed you to lead. Don't conform. Don't sink back into familiarity. I've given you compelling evidence within this book, both externally and within the Word of God, that shows that the arrows have to be reversed. We can't keep doing what we've always done and expect different results. Take the leap of faith, and trust God with the rest.

I want to help you any way I can. You can email me, matt@box.church.

I will be glad to get in touch with you and talk with you and put you in touch who other Pastors who have already chosen to reverse the arrows. If you are not a Pastor but long for your church to reverse the arrows, reach out to me.

I want God's Church to thrive and be released. I want it to function as it Biblically was designed to do. Reverse the arrows and watch God do an amazing work in your life and in the life of His people.

www.ingramcontent.com/pod-product-compliance
Lightning Source LLC
Chambersburg PA
CBHW030813150426
42813CB00069BA/3351/J